Echoes from th[ ] s

The Life and Adventures of [ ] r

Here' & Gods' wild places
His wild critters and a
few "wild" people you'
met along life's trail.
Glen A. Hinshaw

Art
Hope you will enjoy reading
this book as much as I did!
Thanks for being a "big
brother" that I feel I can call
on for so many things. I
really appreciate all the help!
Always
Beth Short

Glen A. Hinshaw

Echoes from the Mountains: The Life and Adventures of a
Colorado Wildlife Officer

Publisher: Glen A. Hinshaw

Author: Glen A. Hinshaw

Cover design and photo: Glen A. Hinshaw

Printed by Createspace.com
Available through Amazon.com and local booksellers

_____

Includes Index
Includes photographs

ISBN - 13:978-1502768117
Title ID 5000419

1. Glen Hinshaw, 2 Colorado, 3, Title, 4 Wildlife, 5 Game
   Warden

_____

A note about the pictures in this book: Most of the pictures are
from the author's personal collection. All other pictures are used
with permission of and credit given to the photographer.

TABLE OF CONTENTS

DEDICATION

I dedicate this book to my dad Leslie Hinshaw who taught me to enjoy, and care about wild places and wildlife. He was my role model in my youth. He introduced me to the mountains of Colorado and the outdoor life and taught me not only how to survive, but to enjoy God's creation.

I further dedicate this book to Beth Short who was my wife during the years that I was a wildlife officer, and to our children Lois and Ralph who lived the high country life with us, and to my wife Carol who has shared these latter years of our lives.

I further dedicate this book to the state and federal game wardens, wildlife conservation officers, district wildlife managers, troopers, game rangers, and every other person who has worn, wears or will wear the badge of a wildlife law enforcement officer, and to their spouses who stand behind them and to the personnel and retired employees of the Colorado Division of Parks and Wildlife who work behind the scenes and whose dedication is just as essential as for those of us who worked in the field.

I further dedicate this book to the many dedicated teachers and professors who teach our young people.

Last but not least I dedicate this book to the memory of those officers, my buddies behind the badge, who have passed on and left a legacy to inspire those who will follow us.

ACKNOWLEDGEMENTS

I want to thank many people who had a role in the writing of this book. I may not have written this memoir if it hadn't been for our daughter Lois who encouraged me to start writing my stories.

Charlene Ameel, Don Bachmann, Mike Blakeman, Harvey Bray, Lonnie Brown, Don Crane, Grant Houston, Arlene Hinshaw Johnson, Lois Hinshaw Jump, Ralph Hinshaw, Richard Kolisch, Paul Koretko, Phil Leggitt, Bob Little, Jack McKee, Chuck Reichert, Mel Rose, Keith Scott, Beth Short, Ella Stevens, Tim Stevens, Brad Wayt, Brent Woodward, and Mike Zgainer
I want to give special thanks to Dr. Bob Walden and Laird Landon Jr. PhD for reviewing the manuscript and to Phillip Thomas PhD for editing this book.

PREFACE

Mountains have always beckoned me. Although I grew up in the big city, I knew early on that the mountain life was for me. When I was a boy, my dad took me backpacking in the wilderness areas of Colorado. Over the years I have followed trails to the heights of tall peaks and into the depths of dark canyons from Wyoming to New Mexico.

Some of those trails were poorly mapped in the 1950s. Trail crews notched and blazed trees to mark the trails that were sometimes indistinct. When the trail forked there was a guide post that indicated my location and how far it was to my destination.

The old trail blazes are about gone now. Today we have GPS, topographic maps, and guide books that describe every detail along every trail. Sadly, technology and information has diminished the wilderness experience and sense of adventure that I remember.

I have been blessed by many people who were trailblazers and guide posts in my life. Some folks briefly crossed my trail and others I've shared the trail with for many years. Too often I failed to respect and appreciate fellow sojourners. I wish I had been a better listener for that would have made me wiser sooner. As wordy as I am, words fail to express my gratitude. "Thank you" just isn't enough.

As a youth I had a desire to live and work in the great outdoors. I learned all that I could about wildlife conservation by reading, and by talking to game wardens and forest rangers. Great teachers inspired me. My parents encouraged me. By the time I was in high school I dedicated myself toward my goal to be a steward of mountains and wildlife as a Colorado Wildlife Conservation Officer.

We make decisions that determine our destiny and the trails that we follow. We may have a general idea of what we are in for and what is at the end of the trail, but we don't know about the unexpected obstacles and opportunities that we will experience. These are the source of life's adventures. I did not live vicariously through other people's experiences. I lived an exciting life.

An echo is an energy wave that is briefly stored and reflected back to its source. A scenic picture echoes memories of sounds, fragrances, events and feelings. Not everyone who sees the same picture necessarily shares the same emotions that image emotes. Our lives are also an echo of our actions. What we do in life reflects back to us and others and people remember us in different ways. Some echoes are memories and others are the fruits of our labors.

In my book *Crusaders for Wildlife* I paid tribute to the forest rangers, game wardens, biologists, fish culturists, ranchers, business people, volunteers, and others who had an important role in restoring our wildlife heritage in Southwest Colorado. *Echoes from the Mountains* is a memoir of my personal experiences about how I got into the wildlife business and my thirty-four year career of living my dream as a Wildlife Officer for twenty-five of those years. The last nine years of my career I served as a Regional Information Specialist, Public Liaison, and coordinated the regional education, watchable wildlife, and volunteer programs for the Colorado Division of Wildlife.

I lived a life that millions of people think they would have chosen. I have written short stores that describe my life as a wildlife officer and career; realizing that thousands of other officers had their unique experiences because of their location and timing. During my c a r e e r I lived in small towns where life was simple and usually quiet. But, just because a town is small doesn't mean life is boring with little going on. To the contrary, an individual can make a difference in the quality of life with just the little things that he or she can do. Some of my greatest enjoyment and reward was contributing what I could to my town, along with what other citizens were doing. It wasn't that I was anyone special, but I just happened to be there when things happened. My family was involved in many phases of my career as we shared life in the high country.

Wildlife officers stand in the gap protecting wildlife from poachers as well as the public that would harm wildlife and wild places. I lived through many adventures with people, horses, and wildlife in some of the most isolated, rugged, and beautiful mountains in Colorado.

Throughout this book I make reference to the Colorado Game and Fish Department, Game, Fish and Parks Department, Division of Wildlife and Parks and Wildlife. Although the name has been changed by the whims of the Colorado General Assembly, the mission to protect, enhance and manage the wildlife for the people of Colorado has never changed since its creation in 1897.

The Game Warden title was changed to Wildlife Conservation Officer (WCO) in the 1954, but many folks will always call us game wardens, and that's okay, because I've been called a lot worse.

The legislature added the State Parks function and it became the Game, Fish and Parks Department in 1963. In 1973 the legislature separated the State Parks from wildlife and changed the name to Division of Wildlife (DOW). The WCO title changed to District Wildlife Manager (DWM) although the position had the same multipurpose function. Through the rest of this book I will refer to the "Division" rather than the agency name used in a particular time period and use Wildlife Officer in most contexts.

To visualize the places I have written about in this book go online to Google Earth.com ©. Search for features such as towns, mountains, and lakes to enjoy the maps, landscapes, and pictures on that website.

I have included many pictures. Some are old and a little fuzzy. Often it was dark or an event too intense for anyone to be taking pictures and some just didn't turn out.

I have included the names of many people and I apologize for having forgotten the names of some folks who crossed my trail who were really important to me. Time has undoubtedly distorted some details, but I've written things the way I remember them. You may not recognize the names of people in my life, but it is my hope that you will remember the same kinds of people in your own life and for whom you owe a debt of gratitude or even forgiveness.

Welcome to my mountains. Join me, relax, and lean back against a log and have a cup of cowboy coffee as we watch the sun setting over the mountains. I'll throw another log on the fire. Enjoy the warm glow of my campfire and listen to the echoes from the mountains, its wildlife, and a few wild people.

CHAPTER 1
The beginning of my life in the wild

My parents Leslie and Birdean Leggett Hinshaw came from farming families south of Wichita, Kansas. They taught school during the Great Depression. In 1937 they moved up from the prairie to Colorado with my sister Arlene. I think dad moved to Colorado not only for a job, which was hard to find, but also because he was hooked on trout fishing. I was born in Denver in August of 1941. I was raised in northwest Denver. We neighbor kids played outdoors most of the time and our imaginations made up for toys our parents couldn't afford to buy. My great outdoors was a vacant lot next door where we boys played war games, cowboys and Indians, and cops and robbers. We didn't have television, but I listened to the Lone Ranger and Roy Rogers on the radio. In the summer the neighbor boys and I pitched a pup tent in the back yard and pretended we were camping out. We slept many a summer night in our make believe camp.

I played baseball and listened to Dizzy Dean broadcasting baseball games when the great players of the 1950s like Yogi Berra, Mickey Mantle, Stan Musial, Peewee Reese, Jackie Robinson, Willie Mays, and many more. I played Old Timers baseball before the days of little league. If we wore our baseball uniforms we got in free to watch the Denver Bears play at Bears Stadium in what is now Invesco Field at the Mile High.

After the war years life was stable in our little neighborhood on West Hayward Place. However, one morning in 1949 my sister Arlene was walking to Lake Junior High School and a neighbor's dog attacked and bit her. The dog had rabies. Having been exposed to the disease, Arlene underwent a series of seven painful shots, but the treatment saved her life. I was only eight years old, but I remember that dog and her suffering and for many years I was afraid of dogs.

When I was thirteen years old my folks sent me back to Kansas to work for my uncle Harold on the Hinshaw family wheat farm near Wellington. Even though we had visited my grandparents and other relatives frequently, I had never seen the rolling prairie with the wheat waving ready for harvest. I had the responsibility for feeding, watering chickens and cleaning the chicken coop. I gathered, candled, crated, and took eggs to a market in Wichita. When we harvested our wheat and took it to the grain elevator, I realized how important farming was to our very existence. Our farm fed thousands of people. The experience that I had that summer gave me a mindset that helped me relate to farmers and ranchers. That summer was the first time I had been away from home.

I experienced how violent weather can be on the prairie. The threat of a tornado forced us to seek shelter in the cellar one night. A tornado missed our farm and touched down in Udall Kansas on May 25, 1955, killing eighty-five people. I'll never forget the impact that had on this Colorado boy, who by comparison had never experienced more than a mountain breeze.

I never got homesick, except for the mountains. Oh, how I longed to be in the mountains. When I returned to Colorado my heart raced when the bus driver announced that we could see Pikes Peak and the Rocky Mountains. I was home again.

I wish you knew my dad

Some of my earliest memories are of sitting with dad, mom and Arlene in church. I accepted Jesus Christ as my Lord and Savior when I was nine years old. Faith and fishing had a lot to do with my destiny. My early childhood experiences in the outdoors gave focus for what would become my life's work. I started fishing with a stick and string when the water from the garden hose created a miniature stream in a row of our victory garden. I caught my first fish at Sloan's Lake when I was three years old and I had an adult fishing license by the time I was eight.

Learning to fish
in the garden
circa 1944

I trailed along with dad rabbit and pheasant hunting with my trusty popgun. He was an expert marksman. He taught me how to shoot a rifle, but I didn't hunt deer and elk until I completed an NRA gun safety class at the Aurora Gun Club

Dad taught me how to rig my fishing rod, cast, tie knots, bait a hook, play a fish and use my Boy Scout knife to gut fish and preserve them. We weren't into catch and release fishing. He took me downtown to Gart's Sporting Goods Store [now Sports Authority] on Larimer Street when it was "skid row" and alcoholics were sometimes passed out on the sidewalk. Dad had a fishing tackle business in the house, so he bought tackle wholesale and sold it retail. He was on a first name basis with the Gart brothers. He outfitted me with hip boots, a fishing jacket, a Goodall spinning reel, willow creel, net, and a waterproof match case. He handcrafted my first bamboo fishing rod.

Dad specialized in making bamboo fishing rods. He taught me to wrap the guides on his rods. We had dozens of men coming to the house to buy rods, reels, and other tackle. Dad made lures and tied flies for sale. I snelled bait hooks and picked up night crawlers from the neighbors lawns; selling them for a penny apiece I earned $45 one summer.I got to hang out with men and listen to their fish stories and secrets. I learned early: *"All fishermen are liars, except you and me and sometimes I'm not so sure about you."*

During the 1940s and '50s we took an annual fishing trip to the Colorado River below Parshall, Colorado. Many of the ranches had primitive cabins along the river that had a wood burning cook stove, table, chairs and beds. An outhouse was just yards away along with a woodpile, and a well with a hand pump. Dad split firewood and carried water in a bucket and mother cooked. Our favorite place to stay was Con's Cabins. Mother cooked and Arlene kept me occupied while dad was out fishing. I wanted to go fishing, but she had me playing house. By the time I

Hunting with dad circa 1944

Arlene watching me "fish" the Colo. River circa 1944

was eight years old I followed dad on the river. He showed me how to read the water and cast my line to where fish waited for food to drift by. The rancher had a daughter my age. I really liked her, probably because she let me ride her horse. I loved the feeling of that horse, but being a city kid I never got to ride another one until I was in college.

Dad always set a good example for me. He asked for permission to fish or hunt on private land. He had a way of being granted permission; maybe because he had been a farmer and spoke their language. After a successful fishing trip we went to the ranch house and showed our catch and offered the rancher some of our fish. Dad had me give him the fish. As a result we sometimes went home without our full bag limits. We did the same thing when we went pheasant hunting. Dad sent Christmas cards and made friends with many landowners. He didn't take them for granted. I was learning from dad how to get along with people.

Dad and I with our limits of big fish circa 1950

Dad was a postal letter carrier who could walk the legs off a good horse. I went on my first backpack trip to Rainbow Lake west of Walden, Colorado when I was nine years old. Dad carried all our gear. I carried a small back pack with some extra socks, raincoat, fishing tackle, and the donuts. Dad loved donuts. We didn't hike just for the fun of it.

Backpacking to Mosquito Lake, Flattops Wilderness circa 1954

Our mission was to find high country lakes and streams loaded with lunker trout.

When we reached the lake, we pitched our pup tent, cut fir boughs to soften the ground (no foam or air mattress), and gathered firewood (no gas stove). We caught fish for supper. Dad taught me how to build a campfire. When it burned down to hot coals, we rolled our fish in corn meal, salted, and fried them. The flavor of those fresh trout still echoes against my taste buds. Instant potatoes tasted like paste, but when you're hungry a dash of campfire ash, salt, and butter made them acceptable. The only dried foods we carried were peaches and apricots. Canned food was too heavy. Freeze dried foods hadn't been invented yet. Breakfast was either bacon and eggs or dried milk, cereal and a donut. Lunch was a chipped beef and cheese sandwich and a candy bar. We drank water from any creek, spring, or lake. We never heard of the parasite Giardia and water filters hadn't been invented yet.

After supper we washed dishes and went back to fishing. When a thunderstorm came over the Divide, we got into our tent and talked about fishing and life. When darkness came we crawled into our army surplus sleeping bags. The rain poured down, lightning flashed and lit our tent like a lantern. Thunder echoed off the surrounding peaks and shook the ground. Dad wasn't scared so why should I? The falling rain lulled me off to sleep. This was the life for me!

As a youth I focused on fishing, but now the echo I value the most is that FISHING WAS NOT A MATTER OF CATCHING FISH, BUT MORE A MATTER OF BEING WITH DAD. I was fortunate to have had a dad who was a good role model and loved the outdoors with respect and awe. He introduced me to the great outdoors and I would come to dedicate myself to protecting it. He taught me the hunting, fishing, and woodsmanship skills that I used and have built upon throughout my life. He was also a role model of honesty and integrity, the foundation of sportsmanship: what a man is when no one is watching.

A Friend Indeed

From its very inception in the early 1900s the Game Warden was solely responsible for wildlife law enforcement. When the Department changed the Game Warden title to that the multipurpose Wildlife Conservation Officer (WCO), it produced a film *A Friend Indeed,* to introduce the diversity the new position. Terrell Quick, a

WCO, starred in the film.   I remember scenes of his going to Colorado A & M [CSU] for his wildlife education, becoming a WCO and then going to work checking fishermen and hunters, riding a horseback patrol, and other duties such as such as game counts, and public relations. The last segment was of Terrell searching for and finding a lost hunter and the closing narrative ". . . he is a friend indeed." I wanted to become the man in that movie.

Dallas Morgan-lion trapper and Game Warden

Dallas Morgan was the Game Warden in Hot Sulphur Springs in the early 1950s. Dad and I met Dallas through a local outfitter in Parshall. We saw Dallas every so often when we were fishing the Colorado River or Granby Reservoir. Dallas was also known for trapping mountain lions. Dallas and dad became friends and he stayed at our house when he brought his lion pelts to the Denver headquarters. I was mesmerized by his lion and game warden stories. One morning he took several lion pelts out of his Jeep and tied them over the hood and drove down to the Game and Fish Department headquarters. Dad and I met other game wardens when we were fishing, but Dallas was only one that I knew. Years later I would. get to tell him how he had influenced me to become a wildlife officer.

The hike that changed my life

By the time I was seventeen years old, dad and I had hiked or jeeped to most of the back country lakes and streams in Colorado north of Interstate 70. I was thirteen years old when dad took me on a twelve mile back pack trip to Dome Lake on the South Fork on the Elk River, north of Steamboat

Dome Lake Mt. Zirkel Wilderness
Photo by Ken Kegener

Springs, Colorado. The trail was intermittent and there were no

topographical maps, no GPS, no cell phones, no rescue helicopters, no airplanes or any other man-made devices or noise - just the sounds of water, wind in the trees, birds, and squirrels. Dad taught me how to keep from getting lost by looking back to where we had come from, and to constantly look around for landmarks so that I could stay oriented. We slept under the stars. At night the clear mountain skies magnified the Milky Way, and the song of coyotes howling echoed across the canyon. The only other person we saw on that trip was Clifford "Bud" Hurd, the WCO in Steamboat Springs. He was on a horseback patrol. After he checked our fishing licenses and fish I asked him what it took to become a WCO. He said, "Young man, you learn how to read, write, think, and get along with people." That good advice is foundational for success in any c a r e e r. I knew the outdoor life in the mountains was for me. I determined on that trip that I wanted to become a WCO. I had high school a h e a d of me and college was a foregone conclusion.

Alpha teachers

An Alpha wolf is the leader of his pack and I learned from Alpha teachers and professors who were a cut above all others. My wildlife education really started when I was at Skinner Junior High in North Denver. The Denver Public School system gave Miss Wheeler, our science teacher, a high level of academic freedom to bring her hobby of herpetology to school. Aquariums and cages were all around the science room that contained reptiles and amphibians including a rattlesnake, coral snake, a gila monster, Satan (a twelve foot boa constrictor) and a variety of "harmless" reptiles and amphibians.

Once a week we dropped a mouse in with the rattlesnake and watched it coil, strike, and eat it. The girls cringed, but I thought it was so cool. Snake night was after school on Thursdays. Those who wanted to participate could handle all the snakes except the poisonous ones. It took four boys to hold Satan, but we didn't get to do that after Bill Tilzey got bit. Bill's mother took him to their doctor to have some snake teeth removed from his hide. There was no complaint, law suit, or any action taken and certainly nothing in the media. Such an event now would make the national n e w s, lawyers would come out of the woodwork, and Miss Wheeler would be fired. Most girls hated that class, but she was a trailblazer to me.

Miss Craig was my homeroom teacher and asked, "Don't you ever read anything besides outdoor books?" Well, at least I was reading and she had us writing book reports. I read every wildlife book I could find in the Denver Public Library. When she gave us other writing assignments I chose to write about wildlife or wild places

Richard Inglis was my favorite biology teacher and he also sponsored a conservation club. We worked on projects with WCOs Terrell Quick and Bob Reynolds building rabbit and quail shelters on the prairie. We drilled holes in the ice at Echo Lake for fish biologist Don Nolting who was doing water chemistry analysis as part of a winterkill research project. We planted a shelter

Mr. Inglis and conservation club with a new picnic table for the Mt. Evans State Wildlife Area circa 1958

belt under the guidance of the Soil Conservation service. We shingled a Forest Service shelter below Mount Evans. We built picnic tables and worked on a stream improvement project on Bear Creek in the Mount Evans State Wildlife Area. Mr. Inglis taught an advanced biology class and with his guidance I designed and conducted a water quality study of Clear Creek from its headwaters where the Eisenhower Tunnel is now, all the way down stream to Denver. I collected and tested water samples, collected flora and fauna specimens and wrote a report on those investigations.

For another project I built a model fish hatchery and wrote two research papers on the history of fish hatcheries and their operations. I interviewed Gene Cook, the supervisor of Colorado's fish hatcheries. He explained how a fish hatchery functioned and the importance of nutrition. He arranged for me to get some fingerling rainbow trout from the Henderson Fish Hatchery for my model hatchery. My project won second place in the science fair.

I had many good teachers and then a few extra special educators; some were in the classroom and some in the real world. Those exposures to professional natural resource personnel furthered my dedication to pursue a career in wildlife management.

Dad was a member of the Denver Metropolitan Wildlife Club and took me to their meetings. I witnessed sportsmen working together with the Game and Fish Department. I knew some of the men in the club after they sponsored one of our conservation club projects. Dad subscribed to the earliest editions of Conservation Comments the precursor to Colorado Outdoors magazine. I read Outdoor Life and Sports Afield magazines from cover to cover. I was hooked on wildlife.

Colorado State University-home of the Rams

The Colorado A&M Aggies had just become the Colorado State University Rams when my parents dropped me off at the Ellis Hall dormitory in the fall of 1959. I was excited to be on my own. The four years ahead seemed like an eternity, but time flies when you're

Studying in my dorm room 1959

having fun. Jim Kellogg and I were classmates throughout our junior and senior high school years, and we were roommates for two years at CSU. Jim majored in range management and I in wildlife management. One of the interests we shared was target shooting. We kept our .22 rifles and ammunition in our unlocked closets. We spent many Saturdays in the foothills plinking and shooting targets.

I enjoyed many activities in addition to academics. I was elected freshman representative of the College of Forestry to the CSU Student Legislature. That was my first experience of being elected to anything. I have always enjoyed sports. I wrestled in high school, but my folks wouldn't let me play football, because I was too small. However, I spent many a Sunday afternoon at one of the city parks joining other boys in a good game of football. There was always room for another player. I tried out for the Forestry College intramural football team that competed with other colleges within the university. It was rough two-handed touch football with no pads, but I loved playing the game. Since I was short I had to be quick to avoid not only getting hurt, but to play effectively. In the spring I played third base fast-pitch softball for the Baptist Student Union. I was active in Inter Varsity, an interdenominational Christian group of students, who gathered weekly for Bible study and prayer. I was elected president of the chapter in my senior year

It was all about learning and growing up

Most of the upper level classes had prerequisites such as math, English, speech, chemistry, physics, botany, soils, geology, zoology, and other basic courses. I hardly put my foot in the door of the forestry building until my junior year. Building upon those foundational courses. I studied physiology, anatomy, mammology, zoology, limnology, and ichthyology. We had specificwildlife courses in ecology, game and fish management,wildlife diseases, law enforcement, technical writing, statistics, management techniques, and public relations.

Learning in the outdoor classroom was a common experience for natural resource students at Pingree Park circa 1962

At the end of my sophomore year I went to forestry camp at Pingree Park Campus. We lived four boys to a cabin that were primitive. Having no electricity, we studied by Coleman lanterns. A wood-fired boiler heated water for community showers. We ate in a dining hall and there was one classroom. The curricula involved range, forest, and wildlife management taught entirely in the field. Forestry camp was more than book learning. We did the work in addition to reading and listen to lectures.

Academics were hard for me. My learning style was more visual that auditory. We spent so much time identifying and memorizing scientific and common names of trees, bushes, grasses, birds, mammals, fish, and other things that are soon forgotten if they're not used. My problem was forgetting half of that stuff the day before final exams. I learned that the most important part of my education was not regurgitating what professors poured into my brain, but expanding my curiosity and ability to keep on learning.

There were two pioneer leaders that have impacted American conservation and our wildlife education. Gifford Pinchot became the first Chief of the U.S. Forest Service in 1905. He had witnessed the destruction of eastern forests and brought his philosophy of *". . . the greatest good for the most people. . ."* Later he added *". . . in the long run."* Pinchot emphasized the extraction and use of natural resources as necessities for life itself. He promoted sustainable forestry practices and pioneered the art and science of forest management in America.

Aldo Leopold is considered the father of modern wildlife management. He earned a degree in forestry from Yale University and went to work for the Forest Service in New Mexico in 1909 where he pioneered in ecological approaches to land and wildlife management. Leopold thought the Forest Service's utilitarian policies were beginning to damage ecosystems and thought correctly that the automobile was beginning to place a growing recreational demand on wilderness ecosystems. He pioneered ecological approaches to land management and he was one of the early advocates for wilderness and proposed the Gila Wilderness become the first wilderness system in lands administered by the Forest Service.

Leopold left the Forest Service after fifteen years in New Mexico and became Professor of Game Management at the University of Wisconsin. In 1933 he wrote our text book Game Management. The opening sentence read, *"Game management is the art of making land produce sustained annual crops of wild game for recreational use."* For decades wildlife agencies have employed Leopold's principles of sustainable harvest of game and fish while maintaining vigorous wildlife populations. We were taught that wildlife and timber were to be managed as commodities. Leopold added an ethical component to resource management that is still employed today. As future wildlife managers we learned from Leopold: *"To keep every cog and wheel is the first precaution of intelligent tinkering."*

Ronald Ryder PhD, Harold Steinhoff PhD, and D o u g l a s "Doug" Gilbert Phd were my major professors. Dr. Gilbert t a u g h t us, "The secret to game management is people management." He taught Public *Relations in Natural Resource Management.* During my thirty-four years as a wildlife professional, I internalized his training and learned how to work with people to benefit wildlife and the environment.

As our society has become more urbanized, it has lost contact with the land and its stewardship. Various interest groups pressure politicians to respond to their needs and values that can put wildlife at risk. Others pressure politicians on behalf of wildlife and that brings conflict. As a result, citizens through our politicians, have caused resource agencies to adapt policies that reflect changing values, which are often more emotional than biologically sound. Although the ecological principles that Leopold expounded are still valid today, the technology has dramatically changed with the advent of computer science. Wildlife management is an art based on science to deal with real world circumstances.

White River elk study

One of the graduation requirements for the Bachelor of Science degree in Wildlife Management was an approved summer of work experience. Between my junior and senior years I worked on the White River Elk Study for the Game and Fish Department. Our crew mapped and evaluated the big game winter range from Rifle to Yampa, Colorado. We lived in tents, ate under a rain fly, showered at truck stops, and sometimes bathed in the Colorado River. It was a great summer.

Our project leader Ray Boyd, a wildlife researcher,

Going to work in our Jeep circa 1962

assigned me to contact ranchers and get permission to cross their properties to access Forest Service and Bureau of Land Management (BLM) land. One day Ray sent me to meet with Orris Albertson, a rancher on Derby Creek who was in a dispute with the Forest Service over water issues he owned on Keener Lake. When I was a teenager Dad and I had backpacked all over the upper Derby Creek drainage in the Flattops Wilderness, so I knew the area. Mr. Albertson invited me into his house. After pouring me a cup of coffee, he told me about his dispute and I understood his position. Knowing that I was just a student, he softened his tone and told me about his ranching heritage. I didn't even have to ask for permission to cross his land. He showed me the access gates.

I met John Benton, a neighboring rancher who told me about his ranching operation and shared his knowledge of range management and pointed out where the elk and deer actually wintered. He helped me gain a perspective that we hadn't been taught in a classroom. The experience of

Bath time in the Colorado River

meeting ranchers, listening to their problems and solutions opened my mind to the fact that these folks knew a lot more about wildlife than what we were led to believe in college. They had lived on the land for generations and respected the land and understood how natural systems worked. I learned a little more about what to include in my thinking process.

While working in the Glenwood Springs area I learned about being gutsy. One day we came in from the field to a truck stop. I saw the Denver Post at a news stand and was shocked to see my mother's picture on the front page, along with her name, age, and address. She was a bank teller when a robber came up to her window and pointed a gun in her face, and told her to "fill the bag." My four foot eleven inch mother placed her hands on her hips a n d defiantly asked, "Does your mother know you're doing this?" After he threatened to shoot her if she pulled an alarm, she put $1,000 in the bag, but didn't give him all the money.

One day three of us who were working on the project, drove to Sweetwater Creek, a tributary of the Colorado River, a short distance north of Interstate 70. I took the Tote Goat [trail bike] to finish mapping an area while my partners took truck to check out a new area. A big thunderhead came over the mountain and I drove down to where we were going to meet. They weren't there, so I drove u p to a ranch house to get out of the rain. Clarence and Alma Stevens invited me into their home. Mrs. Stevens asked me if I'd like to have a bowl of beef stew. We'd been eating peanut butter and jelly sandwiches all summer, so I gladly accepted. She offered me a bowl of homemade ice cream that they had left over from a church social. I hadn't seen a church in the valley, so I asked them where they went to church. I grew up where churches were buildings, preferably with steeples, and a sign out front denoting a denomination. Mr. Stevens said the ranchers in the valley brought their kids to their house for Sunday school and a missionary came once a month to lead them in a Bible study.

That conversation was life changing. We visited for several hours and I realized that church was not a building, but a

The Stevens Ranch House

gathering of people that could meet any place to worship. At the time I was considering leaving CSU and going to a seminary to become a pastor, but a professor at the seminary suggested I finish my degree and reconsider. I finished my degree and doors opened for me to continue my wildlife career. My ministry would become one of leading Bible studies and filling pulpits in small towns and in churches without pastors.

During my senior year our wildlife class went on field trips into the real world to see things first hand that we had been learning. Dr. Gilbert knew that I had a talent for public relations and gave me additional assignments. I enjoyed going to local radio stations and newspapers to give interviews and stories about what these two dozen students were doing in their town. These experiences with real people in their world facilitated part of my transition from being a student to becoming a wildlife professional

Colorado State University
Wildlife Section- Class of 1963

CHAPTER 2
A dream comes true

The blind date that changed my life

I was a sophomore at CSU when the Angels (Rev. and Mrs. Angel) set me up with a blind date on Friday the 13th, January, 1961 with Beth Short, a farm girl from Brighton, Colorado. When I got back to Fort Collins I told my roommate Jim that someday I was going to marry that girl. Not love at first sight mind you, but I just knew. After her freshman year, Beth sacrificed her college attendance at Life Bible College in Los Angeles, California and moved to Fort Collins while I finished my senior year. Although we enjoyed the outdoors together, our relationship was predicated on a strong spiritual connection. When we got married in June, 1963, I had forty-five dollars, no job, but we had no debt.

I had taken written tests for the WCO position with both Arizona and New Mexico who used the same test. When I opened Colorado's written test I realized that I had already taken it twice. After taking the written test we went before an oral review board. One of the questions they asked on the oral test was, "Are you willing to work long hours, weekends, and holidays with no extra pay or time off?" I enthusiastically said, "YES", not knowing what the impact on my family would be

The State Personnel Board didn't send the test results until late summer. To keep the wolf away from the door, I got a job driving a truck for a used clothing store in Commerce City on the northeast outskirts of Denver. I knew my draft board was after me, because I had already passed my physical and was told I would be called up in just a few weeks. All men who attended a land grant college such as CSU were required to take two years of ROTC. The recruiter said that I had an option to apply to Officer Candidate School (OCS) and become an Army officer that required a three year commitment or allow myself to be drafted as a private. I didn't want to make a long term commitment to the military as an officer. The future was uncertain. I was hoping to be hired before I got drafted, because an employer had to rehire you when you returned from military service and I wouldn't have to go through the testing again. One August morning in 1963 we were listening to the Paul Harvey Morning News when he announced, "President Kennedy has declared married men exempt from the draft." The next day I got my draft notice in the mail, and I was reclassified. We were relieved to say the least.

I got the job

The State Personnel Board in Colorado had just begun requiring a Bachelor of Science degree in wildlife management or a related field of study to apply for a WCO position. Only men could apply. Finally, notice came in the mail that I had ranked high enough on the written and oral exams to be hired in September, 1963. It was a dream come true to join the ranks of a hundred WCOs in the Colorado Game and Fish Department. Phil Mason, Don Minnich, Larry Huck, Judd Cooney, and I were issued law enforcement commissions and measured for uniforms on our first day on September 26, 1963, just two weeks before the big game season opened. There was no probation or formal training. We were put to work assembling hunter safety packets and doing other busy work at the Denver headquarters. We received one field assignment to work on an experimental duck season

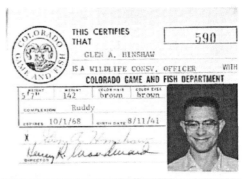

My first wildlife law enforcement commission 1963

in the San Luis Valley. I was assigned to U.S. Fish and Wildlife agent. I just followed him. He was friendly, courteous, and respectful even to the violators that we cited for over bag limits and for killing federally protected birds.

Before the big game season in October, the Department gathered all the WCOs for an inservice training session. Staff updated us on laws and procedures to strengthen state-wide law enforcement uniformity. It was also a social time to renew friendships. Veteran officers welcomed the rookies. I introduced myself to Terrell Quick and Bob Reynolds and thanked them for the time they spent with our high school conservation club. Dallas Morgan remembered staying at our house. I also thanked Gene

Cook for helping me with my biology project. Meeting these men on a professional level gave me a sense of accomplishment as well.

What kind of an outfit was this anyway?

When I went to work many of the officers were World War II and/or Korean War veterans. Some had experienced combat, had been wounded, witnessed unspeakable horrors, and were highly decorated for their military service. Some used the G.I. Bill to go to college and earn degrees in wildlife management. These men were tough, respectful, independent, and fiercely loyal to one another. They looked out for each other and worked together like brothers in an infantry squad. This comradery extended throughout the agency. For those of us who didn't share in their war experiences, they absorbed us into their culture. We were indeed a "band of brothers."

Veteran officers talked about the good old days before two-way radios, paperwork, and meetings. I learned from my supervisor and fellow officers to function independently without a high level of supervision. That is one of the most valued elements of the job. We worked hard, because we wanted to. We didn't punch a time clock. When a challenge faced us, we took care of it. We didn't need to be told what to do very often.

Excellent performance above and beyond the call of duty was the standard expectation, and not worthy of any special recognition. One seldom received praise for a job well done. Merit ratings had not been invented yet. Initiative to envision and do things that hadn't been done before was not only acceptable, but also supported. We operated in a positive environment within the agency. Taking risks was the norm and not measured by the value of the goal, not the cost of failure. We didn't work for just a paycheck, but we focused on doing all we could to protect and conserve Colorado's wildlife heritage. Few careers are as rewarding as those in the field of natural resource conservation in which you find people who love their careers.

Assignment . . . Cortez

We were given a choice of several open districts. I didn't request a specific district, but said that I wanted as far away from Denver as possible. Assistant Director Bob Elliot called us into his office. He assigned each of us to a district. "Glen. . . Cortez." I was happy. You can't get much farther from Denver than that. When I was nine years old our family took a vacation to Mesa Verde. When I was senior our CSU wildlife section took a field trip that included Mesa Verde. I did a radio interview on KVFC AM and provided a story to the Cortez Journal. So, I had a little memory of what the district looked like.

When I told Beth that we were moving to Cortez, her first comment was, "Oh no, all the mountains have lost their tops . . . just flat mesas, but when we arrived I knew that was not the case." She loved mountains too.

Two days before the big game season, we loaded our car and headed across Colorado to Cortez. Our adventurous life was just beginning.

Cortez, Colorado looking eastward to the LaPlata Mountains circa 2014
Photo by Lois Jump

As we drove into Cortez I liked what I saw. I didn't know any of the town's history of boom and bust, but it was a stable community with a diverse economic base of agriculture, oil and gas, and tourism.

Cortez Colorado, population 6,000, elevation 6,000 feet looking northward circa 1963

Cortez was a *Gateway Community* to Colorado and the San Juan Mountains.

Scotty Bessire was my first supervisor. I knocked on his door and introduced myself, "I am Glen Hinshaw." Scotty replied, "That supposed to mean something to me?" I continued that I was the new WCO to replace retiring Harry Terrell. Scotty seemed a little surprised. He invited me into his house and went to the phone and called Bob Elliott. "Who is this kid and what am I supposed to do with him?"

I didn't catch the rest of the conversation, but was beginning to wonder what I'd gotten myself into. Scotty shook my hand and welcomed me and told me to go to the Frontier Motel on the east side of Cortez and they would give me the state rate. He told me he would pick me up the next morning and that I would be riding around with WCO Bill Fischer in Dolores for most of the hunting season.

While I was working that first hunting season, Beth found a furnished one bedroom apartment for forty-five dollars a month. Since I hadn't been paid yet, we didn't have enough money to pay a deposit or the first month's rent. The landlord said we could move in and pay when I got my first paycheck. If forty-five dollars a month sounds like a small sum for an apartment rental, consider that my monthly salary was just $425 a month. That was pretty good pay in 1963. Beth set about making our nest, never knowing when I would be home.

When I went to work, the Division (in my case) got two for the price of one. The culture of the agency included, but did not require wives' participation. Beth fit right into her new role. Like most officers' wives, she answered the phone, took messages, and sometimes had to deal with citizens who were angry with the Division or her husband. The phone calls increased the following year when the Division published our names and hometowns in the big game hunting brochure. The Division intended to help hunters plan their hunting trips by having a local contact but without regard to the stress upon our wives.

He told me since I would be working long hours he expected me to take Beth with me. She said, "Riding along with you was exciting and got me out of the house and it made up for the long hours and your being called out in the middle of the night."

The Four-Corners is big country

The Cortez district was in the four corners of southwestern Colorado where Colorado, New Mexico, Arizona, and Utah state lines meet. The desert of the southwestern United States meets the Rocky Mountains in Cortez, a town of about 6,000 people in 1963. The district boundaries were the New Mexico state line to the south, the Utah state line on the west, and eastward to 13,321 foot Mt. Hesperus in the

Mesa Verde ramparts on the left and the Sleeping Ute Mountain viewed from the LaPlata Mountains

LaPlata Mountains (a subrange of the San Juan mountain range) and most of the country south of the town of Dolores on the north.

The town of Towaoc is headquarters of the Ute Mountain Ute Tribe, nestled on the eastern flank of The Sleeping Ute Mountain, southwest of Cortez. The reservation included lands in the Four Corners of southeastern Utah, northern New Mexico and southwestern Colorado. I had no jurisdiction on the reservation.

The ramparts of Mesa Verde National Park were south of Cortez. This 52,000 acre preserve of Ancient Pueblo Indian ruins is one of the largest examples preserving the works of ancient man in the United States... Although I cooperated with the National Park Service, I had no jurisdiction within the Park.

My responsibilities extended from the sandstone canyons and mesas along the Utah state line eastward to agricultural lands mixed with pinion-juniper forests on up to aspen, pine, spruce-fir, and alpine tundra high in the LaPlata Mountains.

These diverse life zones supported a variety of wildlife including deer, elk, bear, mountain lion, bobcat, raccoon, turkey, pheasant, blue grouse, waterfowl, beaver, muskrat, coyote, red fox, golden eagle, several species of raptors and all the little animals and birds. The Bureau of Land Management (BLM), the San Juan

National Forest and the National Park Service managed the public lands in the district.

I called him Wild Bill

Scotty Bessire supervised all the wildlife officers in the San Juan Basin from Dove Creek to Pagosa Springs. The morning before deer and elk season Scotty picked me up and radioed to Bill Fischer, the officer in Dolores, to meet us at the Dolores Fish Rearing Unit. While we waited for Bill, Scotty introduced me to Foster Barker, the unit superintendent. We shook hands. Scotty told Foster that he was assigning me to work with Bill. Foster shook my hand again and said, "It was nice knowing you kid."

About that time Bill came rolling into the unit in a cloud of dust. He reached across the seat of his pickup, opened the passenger door, I jumped in, shook hands, and away we went up the Dolores River canyon. The rest of the day was a blur. Fence posts went by like a picket fence. Vehicles didn't have seat belts then or I would have strapped myself in.

Bill was a Navy veteran who piloted a Higgins landing craft in several island invasions in the Pacific during World War II. Wild Bill became my mentor, good friend and confidant. He was a n o nonsense officer, but I learned he had a great sense of humor. He pulled a number of practical jokes on me. I was twenty-two years old, immature for my age, and greener than grass.

My first hunting season

On opening morning I rode with Bill. I had no uniform or badge, but I did have my law enforcement commission card. We passed a pickup truck with two elk in the back. Bill whipped a U turn and stopped the hunters to check their elk. The two carcasses were properly tagged, but they hadn't left any evidence of sex so we couldn't tell if they were cows or bulls. They were in violation of the law.

I had never seen a ticket book and knew nothing about statutes or regulations. Bill taught me how to fill out my first citations. At that time Colorado had the Justice of the Peace (JP) system to handle misdemeanor violations. We drove into Dolores and met with the JP in his general store. There was an office in the back that had four chairs. I sat on an orange crate. My knees were shaking. After the preliminaries I told the judge how we came to stop them and discovered the evidence-of-sex violations. The defendants pleaded guilty and were fined $15.00 and $2.00 court costs. One of the defendants apologized to me. He knew I was j u s t a rookie.

Flying low

When someone was reported lost, sheriffs called their local wildlife officer for help, because he had a two-way radio, knew the country, and could request the regional airplane to help in the search. The Dolores County Sheriff had called Bill to help search for a lost hunter. Bill c a l l e d Wayne Russell our Southwest Regional Pilot.

I had never been close to an airplane, let alone flown in one. I was pretty apprehensive as Wayne, rolled the Division's Cessna 185 down the runway and we left the ground to search the

The Division's Cessna 185

Dolores River Canyon. My anxiety increased significantly when we were flying so low that that I had to look UP to see the canyon rim. Wayne had superb flying skills to avoid the invisible downdrafts that can pull an airplane into a mountain. We found the hunter. He was okay. I relaxed on the return flight, having put my faith in Wayne's skill. Before we landed I already looked forward to flying with him again. He was always so cool, calm, and collected.

During that first hunting season when Bill took some time off, I rode with Pat Waters, the officer in Dove Creek. Pat was built like a tall thin cowboy. He talked slow, but thought real fast. Even though it was hunting season we checked fishermen when we saw them. One day we drove by Narraguinep Reservoir west of Dolores. We checked a fisherman who had one fish over the limit and was still fishing. Pat told him the limit was ten and he had e l e v e n. Sarcastically the fisherman asked, "What's one little old fish?" Then he asked Pat if he was going to get a ticket. Pat told him no, but he would have to take one of the fish so that he wouldn't be over the limit. Instead of taking one fish, Pat took two and when asked why he was taking two Pat replied, "Ah what's one little old fish?" Then Pat told him that if he continued to fish he would get a ticket. He gave the two fish to an elderly couple in Dove Creek for their supper. Pat taught me a good lesson that sometimes it doesn't always take a ticket to get someone's attention. Then again, as Bill taught me, some don't listen until you get into their wallets. Throughout my career I was fortunate to learn my trade from some of the finest role models.

A day to remember

What were you doing in the late morning of November 22, 1963? Some of you hadn't been born yet. I was rotating tires on our car when the music I was listening to was interrupted by the announcement that President Kennedy had been shot. I ran into the house to tell Beth. We didn't' have a television set, so we turned our radio on to listen for further news. We sat there staring at the radio when the announcement came that the President was dead. We were stunned, like everyone else in the nation. Who did this? Why? What is going to happen to our country? Still, we felt confident that our government would continue as it had survived other assassinations and threats. There was a sadness that hung over Cortez and the nation.

On my own

Wisely, Scotty didn't turn me loose during the hunting season. After hunting season he gave me the keys to my 1963 four-wheel drive International Scout. It w a s green with a half cab and a two-way radio. I could talk to the Colorado State Patrol dispatcher, the

My first state vehicle a 1963 Scout in Sandstone Canyon

county sheriff and other wildlife   officers.   Communication was unreliable because mountains and canyons blocked radio signals.

My uniform arrived with badges, name tags, western boots, and a Stetson. I was so proud.

I had been on my district for almost a year when I went to the Denver headquarters for my first training session. When we went to Denver we could take our wives in our state vehicles. Beth and I stayed with my folks. Chuck Foster, Assistant Chief of Law

My first uniform and badge 1963

Enforcement, took all the newer officers to the Adams County Sheriff's Department. Deputies taught us investigation techniques such as finger printing, polygraph, photography, collection and preservation of evidence, interviewing techniques, and court procedures. There was nothing related to officer survival. After that session Clyde Slonaker and other Division instructors taught constitutional

Bert Widhalm, Instructor, Chuck Foster, Larry Huck, and Perry Olson in training with the Adams Sheriff's Department   circa 1964

law, wildlife statutes, regulations, arrest procedures, and other subjects pertinent to wildlife law enforcement, but still no officer survival.

We were given new statute books because the laws had been rewritten. I regret throwing my first law book away. According to that outdated law book, game wardens had the authority to ". . . search [without a warrant] all stage coaches, buckboards, wagons, barrels and boxes for illegal game and fish. . ." They also had the authority to keep Indians on their reservations. A game warden was paid one-third of all fines, the Justice of the Peace a third, and the Colorado General Fund the remaining third.

I guess the General Assembly thought a hungry game warden would get after wildlife violators. Even though it was still the law, after 1937 game wardens and Justices of the Peace no longer received any of the fine money. The JP system served the people well, but the county court system replaced it in 1965. Although I was still as green as my Scout, I launched myself with great enthusiasm into my chosen field of wildlife management.

Mt. Hesperus and the Mancos River Canyon in the LaPlata Mountains.   Photo by Lois Jump

CHAPTER 3
Protecting farmers and ranchers

Beaver trapping 101

When I was student working on the White River Elk Study, a rancher asked me to trap some beaver that were plugging up his irrigation ditches. I told him I couldn't and that he should contact his local wildlife officer for help. I got an earful of complaints about that officer. Whether his complaint was valid or not, I determined that I would work with ranchers as much as possible and nobody would be justified in talking about me that way. I learned that beaver can be a nemesis.

Scotty told me I had some troublesome beavers whose dam was washing out a road near the Jersey Jim fire lookout north of Mancos, I called Harry Terrell, my predecessor, and asked him if he would teach me how to trap beaver, because I never had so much as set a mouse trap. Harry started his wildlife career as a trapper and was glad to teach me.

A Connibear trap set.

The beaver creates its habitat. As an aquatic engineer, it chooses a site with abundant food and building materials such as trees, willows, mud and rock. To the consternation of ranchers, it takes advantage of culverts, head gates, canals, ditches, roads, and other structures.

The 1941 Beaver Control Act required the Division to remove troublesome beavers post-haste. The Division hired beaver trappers, but after World War II most of them became game wardens and the legislature changed the statute again. For years trappers had used leg hold traps, but when I went to work most trappers used the humane Conibear trap. I also inherited a live trap. The problem with live trapping was finding a suitable habitat that wasn't already populated with beaver.

Harry taught me to prepare the trap site by tearing out a small area of the mud and stick dam and place a trap in the breach. When the beaver inspected its impoundment it saw the breach, went into the trap and when it hit the trigger, SNAP! - killing it instantly! I set six traps that afternoon and when I went back the next morning I had caught six beavers. "Nothing to this beaver trapping," I said to myself. I never had such luck ever again. Some ranchers wanted the beaver removed from Sandstone Canyon in what is now the Canyon of the Ancients National Monument. Beaver d a m s were flooding the grass that their cattle were grazing upon. I drove almost to the Utah state line and up Sandstone Canyon. Two-hundred foot tall sandstone

My first beaver

walls echoed every sound. I discovered ancient Indian petroglyphs carved on a rock wall depicting a hunting scene with deer, bighorn sheep, elk, turkey, and blue grouse. I felt like an explorer stepping back in time. I turned my attention to trapping beaver. I could understand why the ranchers wanted the beaver removed where they were flooding grass, but I also saw the benefit the beaver were accomplishing, by raising the water table on the canyon floor. In the long run the dams would increase the vegetation and stabilize the soil. I caught most if not all of the beaver in the canyon. I didn't have to skin the beaver, but took them to the freezer at the Dolores Rearing Unit and a fur buyer bought them from the State. I trapped about a hundred beaver in my first year.

This job is a real blast

When beaver flooded agricultural land, the dam had to be breached and the land drained. Tearing a beaver dam apart by h a n d is a major task. Bill taught me to use dynamite to blow beaver d a m s. I punched holes into the dam with a steel bar and inserted five sticks of dynamite about a foot apart. I gently placed a blasting cap and fuse in the last stick. The fuse burned about a foot a minute so a five foot fuse was all I needed to reach cover.

Scotty called one day and told me to blow a beaver dam that had flooded a small horse pasture on Chicken Creek about a mile north of Mancos. I went to the hardware store in Dolores and bought five sticks of dynamite, a cap, and fuse. I didn't even have to sign my name to purchase explosives. I followed the procedure that Bill taught me. When the dynamite exploded it blew a ten foot hole in the dam. The pasture was drained in minutes.

A week later, Scotty called again and said that the beaver had rebuilt the dam. "Use more powder this time," and he hung up. I was left pondering how much is "more?" So I went back to the hardware store and bought

Placing a cap and fuse into a stick of dynamite

twenty sticks of dynamite, a cap, and fuse. When that dynamite exploded the whole beaver dam nearly went into orbit. When the noise and concussion hit Mancos, some folks probably thought the Russians had attacked. The beaver didn't rebuild the dam and I never again used that much dynamite to blow a beaver dam.

KABOOM!

Arnold the trapper

Officers had the responsibility to oversee the fur trappers in their districts. I inventoried and tagged every shipment of pelts that went out of state. At that time trappers could trap beaver only on private land. All beaver had to be tagged. When the Wildlife

Commission changed the trapping regulations to allow trappers to take beaver on public lands, district officers recommended the number of beaver that could be trapped in each drainage. I didn't have to trap beaver as often after trappers could trap on public land.

The most memorable trapper I ever worked with in Cortez was Arnold, a very experienced trapper who worked hard at his craft. If it walked, Arnold could catch it. He earned a reputation among landowners for trapping nuisance beavers, muskrats, badgers, raccoons, fox, coyotes, and bobcats. He was a master beaver skinner. Arnold got some bad information that skunk pelts were going to bring a big profit. He trapped about twenty. I dreaded the day he called for me to tag his pelts. The smell was nauseating and he quit trapping skunks. Arnold made top dollar for his furs.

Throughout Colorado's history rural families trapped furbearers to supplement their incomes during the winter months. There will always be families that depend on their gardens, livestock, deer, elk, fish and game birds for their food. Colorado citizens passed a constitutional amendment in 1998 that banned most trapping. That initiative brought an end to the trapping business, a source of income for rural families, and an important wildlife management tool.

Game damage

Farmers, fruit growers, gardeners and other agriculturists have problems with wildlife damaging their investments and production of their crops. Most landowners took care of their own predation problems by killing coyotes, foxes, bobcats, raccoons, skunks, and other predators. Sometimes they asked for my help like the farmer who called and said a hawk was killing his chickens. His daughter had taken a hunter safety class and learned that at that time some hawks were protected and some were not. He didn't want to violate the law. I asked him what kind of a hawk was killing his chickens and he answered that it was a "chicken hawk." Taxonomically speaking, there is no such bird.

I appreciated his respect for his daughter and his wanting to obey the law. I gave him permission to kill the hawk, but he would have to turn it over to me. The next day he called and I went out to his farm where he had killed a red-tailed hawk, which was a common species. Along with the hawk laid two dead chickens and feathers all over the chicken coop. Although the hawk was a protected species, it was just common sense to take the hawk and go my way.

In 1937 the Colorado General Assembly began requiring the Game and Fish Department to pay farmers and ranchers from the game cash fund (which comes from hunting and fishing licenses) for the crop damage caused by elk and deer, and livestock losses caused by bear and mountain lion. In order to reduce the amount of money being paid to farmers and ranchers, wildlife officers were assigned to handle the game damage complaints.

The Cortez district had many ranches and farms where game damage occurred. I had no training or experience with game damage, so I relied upon Scotty for guidance. Usually, killing a few deer or trapping a bear or mountain lion stopped the killing. Scotty gave me a State kill permit to kill marauding deer. The Division issued me a 30-06 rifle and ammunition.

You meant to do me right, but you did me wrong

Eleanor Galloway lived down McElmo canyon at the mouth of Trail Canyon west of Cortez. She called about deer eating her cantaloupe. As with many of her neighbors, a garden provided an important income from the local markets. At that time the Division had not provided deer fencing to prevent crop damage.

I got a kill permit from Scotty. Miss Galloway instructed me over the phone. I'm sure I understood her to say, "Go in through the first gate on your left after you cross the McElmo Creek Bridge and there is an electric fence and you go up the right side of the electric fence and shoot the deer." All of the damage control was done at night when the marauding deer fed on only the finest cantaloupe. I had an aircraft landing light mounted on top of the truck cab. When that spotlight hit on a deer, it froze in its tracks and was an easy target for a clean kill. I followed her instructions, but did not see a single deer that night.

I went home and about five o'clock the next morning the phone rang and it was Miss Galloway, "Mr. Hinshaw, I know you meant to do me right, but you have done me wrong! You drove all over my cantaloupe patch and did more damage than the deer." Then it dawned on me what that funny popping noise was while I searched for deer. I didn't know what a cantaloupe patch looked like, but I did then. I should have driven up the left side of the electric fence, not the right side. I drove down and apologized. She gave me a cantaloupe, a watermelon, and some tomatoes out of her garden. Even though I had caused her loss, I experienced her understanding and forgiveness.

A neighboring farmer heard about my escapade through Miss Galloway's cantaloupe patch. He was having deer damage and told me that he needed help, but that he would go with me to show me where to drive. I went out with him and I killed a couple deer. The deer kept coming in, but I couldn't kill them because they ran off when they heard me coming.

ZON gun

One night Beth and I were going down to shoot some deer and as we got to the edge of Cortez city limits came across a motorcycle/car head on collision. The call came over the radio as we stopped. I turned on my flashing red lights. Two boys on a motorcycle were dead at the scene. I had never seen such carnage. I knew they were dead, so I directed traffic until the city police and a state patrolman arrived. The scene was traumatic and one that would be repeated during my career. We turned around and went home. I couldn't stand anymore blood that night.

I made another plan. I figured that deer feared the sound of gunshots, so I got three Zon guns and a gross of cherry bombs and M-80 firecrackers. A Zon gun amplifies an explosion made when water is dripped into a container of carbide which produces acetylene gas. Pressure built up and triggered a flint and steel that made sparks which ignited the acetylene and KABOOM! It was as loud as a 75 millimeter howitzer. I placed three Zon guns facing Trail Canyon where the deer were coming from. I inserted 144 firecrackers into fuse ropes that burn about a foot an hour. I got everything started up and went home.

The next morning about five o'clock the phone rang. (Why did everyone in McElmo Canyon call me at 5:00 in the morning?) "Mr. Hinshaw, did I wake you up?" I answered, "Yes." He said, "Good. Your noise makers kept me awake all night. It sounded like a war down here. I know you are trying to protect old Bill's cantaloupe patch, but we gotta get some sleep."

Unbeknown to me I had aimed the three Zon guns into a grove of trees and shrubs; not knowing his house was behind them. The continual barrage echoed off the canyon walls louder than an artillery battle. I removed the Zon guns that morning.

Beth often went with me, drove the Scout and operated the spotlight. When I killed a deer, she held a leg while I gutted the animal. She helped me load the carcass and I donated the meat to welfare recipients. We never let any meat go to waste. Those echoes from McElmo Canyon remind me of forgiveness and to laugh at myself. A few years after I left Cortez, the Division supplied deer proof fencing for orchards and gardens that prevented deer damage rather than killing the animals.

The Pinto Bean Capital of the World

Montezuma and Dolores counties had thousands of acres planted with pinto beans. Dove Creek, Colorado claims the title "The Pinto Bean Capital of the World". Hundreds of deer lived in the canyons and pinion-juniper forests adjacent to those fields. Most farmers tolerated a few deer feasting on their beans, but when the loss became excessive we started getting game damage complaints.

Scotty told me that one bean farmer near Pleasant View wanted to file a game damage complaint. I drove up to a farm house and was greeted by an old farmer. He took me to his field to show me the damage. I didn't know what a pinto bean pod even looked like. The beans had been cut and windrowed to dry. Later they would be combined to separate the beans from the pods.

Deer tracks were on every square foot of the field. How could anyone tell how many beans the deer had eaten? Surely they had been eating beans, but I had no idea how to settle a claim. Gullible as I was, I asked him, "Be honest with me; do the deer really eat on you all that much?" He answered, "Well young fella, yeah they eat on me now and then . . . course I eat on them now and then too." I asked him if we were about even. He laughed and said that he was probably ahead. I suggested we call it even and he not submit a claim. He agreed. On the way home I felt satisfied that I had saved the sportsmen of Colorado a lot of money. Then it dawned on me that I had actually given him permission to continue poaching deer whenever he needed the meat, which was what he had been doing all the time anyway and would continue to do anyway.

The Cherry Creek deer shoot

A wheat farmer southwest of Durango was claiming deer damage to his winter wheat. Every winter deer moved into that area from the LaPlata mountains. The green wheat was a little more inviting than their normal diet of sagebrush and other browse plants. There were many cold nights that Allison Mason, the officer in Durango, and I drove to the farmer's field. We saw dozens of deer. Allison ran the spotlight and I did the shooting. Allison could gut a deer in the dark with his eyes closed. Over that winter I personally shot nearly a hundred deer in that one field. When Allison didn't go with me, Beth went with me to drive and operate the spotlight. The surviving deer ran off into surrounding canyons and the next night there would be just as many. I don't know that we even made a dent in that population, but as long as we were killing deer the farmer was happy. We often hauled a pickup load of deer to the Durango Fish Hatchery, where they were skinned and meat donated to welfare recipients.

It was a privilege to work with Allison. Two of his sons Phil and Russ were career wildlife officers. For several years Phil was my neighboring officer in the Lake City district when I was in Creede. Phil was killed in the line of duty in September, 2001 when a half-ton roll of bailed hay fell, crushing him to death at the Beaver Creek State Wildlife Area (SWA) west of Gunnison, Colorado. After his tragic death, the Cebolla State Wildlife Area near Lake City was renamed The Mason Family SWA in honor of Allison and his sons.

Game damage control was a major activity in some districts until the Division, in cooperation with landowners, authorized special hunting seasons on private land to have hunters reduce the game damage. In addition the Division has spent millions of dollars to provide ranchers and farmers with game damage materials to fence haystacks, orchards, and other agricultural investments. In the1990s the Division initiated the Wildlife Habitat Partnership program with landowners, the Forest Service and BLM to better manage private and public lands for the benefit of agriculture and wildlife.

Deer repellant

Before the Division supplied deer proof fencing, fruit growers in Montezuma County had deer damage problems. Deer living in the adjacent canyons and draws invaded their orchards. In the fall the bucks rubbed their velvet covered antlers against young trees which scrapped the bark, damaging or killing them. In order to save the trees and game damage claims, I sometimes killed the bucks. I shot at the does with a shotgun loaded with bird shot and cracker shells to scare them off.

Scotty gave me some deer repellant made from concentrated lion urine to spray some young fruit trees in one orchard. Beth drove the Scout while I stood in the back and sprayed the trees. I couldn't help getting some of the spray on myself and the truck. The smell was so bad that the filling station that serviced and washed our state vehicles told me not to come back. We returned that night to check on the orchard. The deer were bedded down where we had sprayed. Chemical repellents and noise makers were seldom effective deterrents to hungry deer.

The blood bath

When the legislature classified bears and mountain lions as game animals it required the Division to pay ranchers for the loss of livestock caused by bears or mountain lions. A woolgrower reported a bear had killed some of his sheep. Since I had no experience with bears killing sheep, I called a federal trapper to go with me to investigate the claim. Sometimes coyotes killed sheep and a rancher would claim that a bear or lion made the kill and try to collect damage payments from the Division.

The rancher provided horses for us to ride to his sheep allotment in the LaPlata Mountains northeast of Mancos. He led us into a patch of aspen where the sheep were bedded down when the bear attacked. I counted twenty-three dead sheep. The scene was a bloodbath; blood splattered all over the trees and grass. It was obvious that the bear attacked and just went to swatting, biting, and ripping through the flock. The trapper set his traps and caught the bear when it came back to feed on the carcasses. The killing stopped. The trapper taught me how to tell the difference between bear, lion, coyote and other predatory kills. I recommended paying the damage claim

CHAPTER 4
Catch me if you can

Wildlife law enforcement is one of the more visible aspects of wildlife management. Lest a reader get the wrong impression, most people who hunt and fish are true sportsmen and women who demand and support wildlife laws. In some places there was a cultural aspect to wildlife law enforcement. During the Great Depression and for years afterward, some families lived off the land. If it hadn't been for killing wildlife, they would have starved. A fishing or hunting trip was fun, but it was more important to put meat on the table. It was okay to kill wildlife as long as it was used and not wasted. (Food stamps and other government welfare programs have removed the justification for poaching.)

Stake out
One of the problems in districts that had deer was spotlighters. Bill called me to go with him for my first stake out one night. We drove north of Dolores and parked where we could observe deer feeding close to the road. We sat in his pickup watching and waiting for a spotlighter to come by.

Bill asked, "You bring anything to eat?" I answered, "No." He reached behind the seat and brought out a grocery bag full of Cedaredge Bing cherries. I love Bing cherries. We sat there half the night and nobody even drove by, but I kept eating those addictive cherries. The next day Bill called the house and asked Beth where I was and she answered, "He's in the bathroom and I don't think he's going anywhere today."

I took Beth with me on some stakeouts. She learned how to operate my two-way radio so she could call for help if need be. We didn't have television and so after dark we just drove out to a likely place to watch for spotligihters. Not exactly a romantic way to spend an evening. Going out on a hunch was seldom productive. Stakeouts and patrolling in the right places and time based on information was usually more productive.

I read it in the newspaper
It didn't take very long for the grapevine to start working for me. A wildlife officer's grapevine is his eyes and ears that keep him informed about wildlife crimes. The Division emphasized that we be seen and make as many hunting and fishing contacts as possible, which necessitated being visible to the public. Poachers, on the

other hand, avoid committing their crimes when there might be witnesses.

One day a boy who had been in one of my hunter safety classes, called to report a possible violation. It was summer and he had been riding on top of a house being moved down a county road. From his perch he saw an elk hide off the side of the road. He returned and found a fresh elk hide, some bones, and a hatchet. I drove to the scene and found what he described, plus a bloodied newspaper. Out-of-town subscribers received their papers by mail. The suspect's name and address were clearly printed on the front page.

I got a search warrant and called officers Allison Mason and Millard Graham for backup. We found an elk in the suspect's freezer. We arrested him and took him to court. The judge fined him the going rate for illegal possession of an elk. The convicted poacher asked me how we had caught him. I told him, "I read it in the newspaper."

He considered wildlife as a source of meat and that he had to pay the "meat market" once in a while. I had caught him hunting pheasants out of season the year before. He owned a successful business and certainly didn't need the meat. To him poaching was a game, but the loss of one's integrity and respect is at a greater cost than the price of meat.

Honest hunters make mistakes

I worked alone on the opening morning of my second hunting season. I had just started out when Scotty radioed for me to meet him at the Fire Lookout. A hunter reported that he'd accidentally killed a cow elk. There are some hunters who having made such a mistake would have walked off and left the carcass to rot. Scotty asked me how I was going to handle the case. I told him that I'd find out what happened first and then decide.

The hunter took us to the dead elk that he had dressed out. He explained that he jumped a herd of elk and shot at a bull, but hit a cow instead. He was distraught. He asked me what I was going to do with him. I said that first I wanted to shake his hand and complimented him for his honesty and having the courage to turn himself in rather than let the animal go to waste. I didn't know about any department policy on how to handle the situation. Scotty didn't say a word all that time. Should I give him a ticket or not? I told the hunter that I wouldn't give him a ticket and that I'd donate the animal to a needy family. He tore his elk license in half and said, "I've killed an elk and I'll not hunt for another one." Scotty didn't say anything until I asked him if that was the way he wanted me to handle the situation. Then he said that if I'd proceeded to issue a ticket, he would have intervened. Later in the 1990s the Division's policy required us to issue tickets to hunters who turned themselves in, so a judge could decide the matter.

Scotty was a patient supervisor. He was riding with me one day and I was driving too fast down a wash-board gravel road. I took a curve too fast and almost bounced out of control. Rather than chew me out for driving too fast he drawled, "Ah, ya can't hit 'em [bumps] all." I slowed down.

They stole my elk

Carl Leonard and I were classmates at CSU. He was stationed in Rocky Ford, Colorado and assigned to help me during the 1964 and 1965 hunting seasons. Prairie wildlife officers often helped mountain officers during the big game season and we helped them during the waterfowl season. One evening we were checking hunters coming off of Haycamp Mesa south of Dolores. The Cortez dispatcher called and said that a license agent in Mancos had reported that a hunter, who was all covered in blood, had come into his business and bought an elk license. A few hunters took a chance at hunting without a license and then after they killed an elk or deer, they'd go buy a license. This practice became serious enough that the Division later required license agents to stop issuing hunting licenses at midnight before the season opened. The dispatcher gave me the number of the elk license.

Soon after that the dispatcher called again; reporting that someone had stolen his elk and he knew where it was. Stealing an elk is a felony in Colorado. Carl and I left our check station and headed for the hunting camp. The hunter said he shot a bull and tracked the wounded animal until he found it dead in a meadow. Someone else had cut his elk's throat. Our informant dressed it out and went back to camp to get his buddies to help him load it up and take it to their camp. When they returned, the elk was gone and they followed the vehicle tracks to a nearby camp.

Carl and I thought we surely had a case. The hunter rode with us to the camp, but stayed in my truck. It was about 9:00 P.M. when we rousted our suspects out of their warm sleeping bags. One could say I interrogated them under duress by having them stand out in the cold in their long-johns. A young man admitted to killing the elk. I checked the tag and license and all was in order.

I asked him to tell me about his elk hunt. This was his first elk hunt. He was watching a meadow when a bull elk walked into the clearing. He shot it in the neck and dropped it. He cut the throat and was so excited he didn't dress it and went back to camp to get his buddies. When they returned they discovered someone else had dressed the elk. They didn't notice that the bull had already been shot. They loaded the elk and took it to camp. Well now, whose elk is it? This case was easily solved when the informant said that he was ashamed of making a poor shot and that the young man should have the elk.

All we had to do then was check a big buck deer hanging next to the elk that his hunting companion had killed. I checked his license and carcass tag and all was legal. Then he produced an elk license with the number that had been reported by license agent in Mancos. He had killed his deer which explained the blood. He still had time to hunt and since his buddy had killed an elk, he thought he would hunt for an elk. Disappointed and yet glad that there were no violations, Carl and I packed it in for the night.

Eyes in the lookout

One of the best times to contact hunters was in their camp at night after they have returned from the day's hunt. Most hunters were tent camping and had a campfire. When the forest was dry, the Forest Service manned the Jersey Jim fire lookout. The smoke-spotter knew that country like the back of her hand. She spotted the smoke from campfires and showed me on a map where the camps were and how to find them. I showed up in many a hidden camp and the hunters asked how I ever found them

I just pointed to the sky and answered, "Someone up there told me you were here."

Jersey Jim Fire Lookout

The sheriff was a racist

Martin Luther King Junior had led a march of over 3,000 people from Selma to Montgomery, Alabama in the spring of 1965. This marked a political and emotional high point of the battle for civil rights. This was in the news, but far away from western Colorado. I grew up in a multi-ethnic neighborhood in North Denver in the 1950s and I had only read about racial segregation in the south.

In the 1965 hunting season I checked a hunting camp from Alabama. As I walked into the camp, a black man, dressed as a butler greeted me with a friendly deep southern drawl. A hunter walked out of the tent and introduced himself as a sheriff from Selma, Alabama.

Just to make conversation I asked the sheriff what he thought about segregation. He said, "I don't have anything against "niggers". "Everybody ought to *OWN* (emphasis added) at least one!" I was shocked and disgusted at his answer. I looked over at his butler and he just hung his head. I've wondered what feelings he had, not interpreted by today's norms, but deep in his heart in 1965. I checked the party's hunting licenses and went on my way. I didn't belong in their world or them in mine.

I was too naïve to be scared

Many times in my career I should have been scared out of my wits, but was too naïve to accept the danger I was in. One night I stopped at a hunting camp. I got out of my Scout and as I approached the tent I identified myself. When the tent flap opened I was looking down the barrel of a pistol. I told the man, "Ah, put that down", and he did. It was probably a good thing I wasn't armed o r he might have shot me. He meant to scare me, but in my youthful innocence was invincible – ha! Some might consider I was brave or courageous, when in fact I was downright stupid. My guardian angel was probably shaking his head and asking God for a new assignment. I know now that I kept him busy.

That same season I was driving down a jeep trail and saw a young hunter walking toward me. Along with his 30-30 I noticed that he was packing a six-gun in a quick-draw holster. I got out of my Scout. When he recognized who I was, he reached down and slipped the holster's leather thong off the hammer. When I asked for his hunting license, he handed it to me. Everything was in order. I kept a close eye on his pistol and his hands. When I finished my contact I said, "You'd better put the thong back on your pistol or it could fall out of its holster." I just wanted to let him know I had seen him slip the thong off the hammer. I wouldn't have known what to do if he had pulled his gun on me.

One winter afternoon I was patrolling southwest of Cortez and observed three young men hunting rabbits. I contacted them when they returned to their truck. One young man didn't have a hunting license. As I was filling out his ticket I noticed one of the hunters was pointing his shotgun at me. As I finished writing the ticket and had the chap sign his name, I asked the other hunter, "You planning to shoot me?" He immediately lowered the shotgun.

In those days we had never heard the phrase "officer survival" We didn't even have what was called an "incident report" to document these kinds of encounters. Wildlife law enforcement officers face situations that urban police and troopers don't experience as often. We contacted more people with guns and knives than any other kind of lawmen. Even though many sportsmen are armed, they are law abiding citizens. Therefore, we could be complacent and slow to react to the threat that an armed person might otherwise pose to other law enforcement officers. We often worked in isolation with limited radio contact and backup was a luxury we seldom had. I never thought of being lucky to have survived. I think God gives wildlife officers a special kind of grace and extra guardian angels.

I caught them in the act of doing nothing

A lot of deer lived along the Summit Ridge Road between Mancos and Dolores. There were just a few ranch houses along the road and very little traffic at night, so spotlights couldn't be seen or shots heard. One night I decided to go out alone and stake out the road. I hid off the road. I had snacks, but no Bing cherries. About two o'clock in the morning an old pickup truck came up the road very slowly. After it passed, I coasted down to the road with my headlights off until the truck was out of site over a small hill. I turned my headlights on and proceeded to the top of the hill, turned my lights and engine off and coasted to a stop. The brake lights came on and they stopped in the middle of the road. A big four-point buck was frozen in their headlights. Both doors slowly opened. My heart raced as I anticipated catching them in the act of poaching a deer. Then one of them reached down, picked up a rock and threw it at the deer, whistled, and watched as the deer jumped the fence and disappeared into the darkness. I must admit to some disappointment after waiting hours for some action and it came down to this.

I decided to make the best of it and caught up with them, turned on my blinking red lights, and they stopped. I approached the truck and greeted the two surprised gents. I told them that I had observed their actions. At first the driver was angry telling me they weren't poachers. I told him I knew that, but just wanted them to know, so they could tell folks that the game warden was out at two o'clock in the morning and if they would have been poaching I would have caught them. He thanked me for being out protecting the deer and that he would tell everyone he knew. So, the night wasn't a total waste.

Bleeding firewood

Wildlife can survive when a community supports not only its existence, but also its well-being. I learned early in my career that many citizens abhorred wildlife being taken illegally and wanted to help in some way. I got phone calls from ranchers, farmers, sportsmen and other law enforcement agencies who reported wildlife violations.

Late one night I got a call from the dispatcher that a State Highway Patrolman had a vehicle stopped and requested that I respond to a possible wildlife violation. I drove east of Cortez on U.S. Highway 160 near the entrance to Mesa Verde National Park. The patrolman had stopped a pickup for a burned out tail light. The officer pointed to blood that was dripping onto the highway. It was a bad case of bleeding firewood. I had him unload his firewood revealing a freshly killed deer. The hunting season was closed. I seized the deer. As he reloaded his firewood I wrote him a citation for unlawful possession of a deer. Law enforcement officers in rural areas particularly, work together. Although we had our specific jurisdictions, we had the authority to enforce any and all of Colorado's statutes.

Bomb scare

The radio crackled, "All peace officers report to the Cortez High School immediately," I quickly drove to the school and joined police, sheriff's deputies, and State Highway Patrolmen. Someone had reported that a bomb was in the school. The Chief of Police assigned each of us a section of the school to direct evacuation of students and search for a bomb.

I went to my assigned hallway and directed each teacher to evacuate his or her students. When we had all the students out of the school we began searching for a bomb. We looked at each other and collectively wondered, "What does a bomb look like?" None of us knew what we were looking for. I guess you know one when you see one or it explodes in your face. Fortunately, no explosives were found and the incident was declared a hoax.

The killer didn't have a fishing license

Allison Mason and I were checking fishermen in the Silverton district in August of 1966. The Wildlife Commission had established fly and lure only fishing regulations for Little Molas Lake. We hid my truck and looked for bait fishermen. We saw a young man down in the creek fishing with a stick, string, and a hook. He gave up and walked to his truck. When he came down the road we stepped out of hiding and stopped him. I asked for his fishing license, and he s a i d he didn't have one and was only trying to catch something to eat. I got smart with him and said that we could arrange for him to have something to eat in the Silverton jail. I don't remember whether it was something that Allison said or just a mutual feeling, but we decided not to press him. We were both unarmed.

Since he was no threat to the fish population we gave him a warning and told him to go on his way. As he pulled away I noted the rear license plate was different than the front. I think the front plate was from Wisconsin and the rear plate from Michigan. I copied the license number and when we got back to my truck I tried to radio the State Patrol dispatcher in Durango. By the time we found a place to call out we didn't know which way he went. My request to the dispatcher for a "wants and warrants" came back negative for Colorado. The National Crime Information Center (NCIC) was new and out of service, so we didn't know if there were any warrants for his arrest. Court records later revealed that he was hiding out in the area and avoided detection. Allison and I had no idea of the potential danger we faced.

A couple weeks later the State Patrol issued an All-Points Bulletin (APB) to be on the lookout for a missing couple from Arizona. In the early fall the couple's pickup camper was found at the bus station in Del Norte. Authorities developed the film in their camera and found pictures of the Lime Creek Campground near

Little Molas Lake inside their blood splattered camper. That information led investigators to the campground where they found the bodies and their little dog in a campground outhouse. A bus station employee identified the suspect who left the truck and bought a bus ticket.

The FBI tracked him down in Michigan. When they arrested him he had the .45 caliber semiautomatic handgun that was used in the murders and he kept it on the seat of his truck. He w a s extradited to Colorado, convicted of first degree murder, and sentenced to life in prison. I later asked Allison about our encounter and he said, "Maybe if we would have pressed him, he would have killed us instead of those folks." I agreed and avoided getting smart with anyone after that experience. Treating people with respect no matter the circumstance is a part of getting along with people and officer survival.

CHAPTER 5
The secret to managing wildlife

"The problem then, is how to bring about a striving for harmony with land among a people many of whom have forgotten there is any such thing as land, among whom education and culture have become almost synonymous with landlessness. This is the problem of conservation education."
Aldo Leopold,   A Sand County Almanac

The Colorado Constitution declares that the people of the State of Colorado own the wildlife within its borders and is held in trust for them by the State. The Division of Wildlife was created in 1 8 9 7 to protect and perpetuate our wildlife heritage. The challenge of managing our wildlife is one of working with the people. The diverse demographics of the state bring opposing value systems into the forefront. Historic agriculturally based communities and urbanites have different perspectives about the land and wildlife. From its early beginning the Division has emphasized wildlife education in schools and informing the public about wildlife issues.

Hunter safety
The number of hunters in Colorado increased dramatically after World War II. The number of gunshot fatalities also increased. The Division adopted a National Rifle Association hunter education program in 1958. Regional Information Specialists taught district officers and volunteers to be instructors. Many school districts offered hunter safety courses as part of their physical education curriculum.

Hunter safety training was not required to obtain a hunting license until a tragic and well publicized hunting accident in 1970. The General Assembly passed a statute requiring anyone born after January 31, 1949 to complete the course before purchasing a hunting license. As the years rolled on all hunters would eventually have taken the course.

Cortez teachers Paul Crawford and Bob Wilson taught me how to teach the course by taking one from them. I was certified as an instructor and began teaching hunter safety classes. The curriculum centered on handling firearms safely, hunting ethics, responsibility, survival, and wildlife laws. At the end of the course each student was required to fire ten .22 caliber rounds at a target and demonstrate safe gun handling.

I've taught many hunter education classes, but one of the most memorable was one I taught in the Mancos school. When it came time for the shooting segment I told the school principal I needed to "shoot some kids." He must have had a rough day as he raised the window blind, looked out on the playground and asked me how many I needed and if I wanted them moving or sitting still.

The only place I could find to "shoot the kids" was in an empty basement room in the VFW hall. Since

Teaching Hunter Safety

the lighting was poor I strung an electric cord with a light bulb hung over the backstop to illuminate the targets. Everything went smoothly. The kids were doing everything I'd taught them. Then one of the students fired and the light went out. The shooter didn't hit the light bulb, but shot the electric cord in half. The purpose of the class wasn't to teach marksmanship, but the safe handling of firearms. Some students were already good marksmen. One night I caught some boys spotlighting deer. One of my students had shot a deer right between the eyes. Nevertheless, the Division's nationally recognized hunter safety program began to reduce the number of gun accidents and fatalities. Hunting has become one of the safest outdoor sports in the nation.

Now hear this

I got the idea of having a weekly radio program after hearing WCO Bill Roland's program on the Craig radio station when dad and I were on a fishing trip. I had done one radio program with Doug Gilbert when I was at CSU and radio interviews on our senior spring trips. Radio station KVFC AM welcomed my proposal. I did some broadcasts with Dottie Wayt and other hosts. I wrote questions

That I was prepared to answer, but once in a while the conversation expanded beyond my preparation.

On one program, Dottie shared her recipe for cooking fish in an automatic dish washer (don't use soap). The result was a fine tasting 'poached' fish. We had a good laugh when I said that as a game warden, I wasn't sure I should eat a poached fish. We usually talked about such things like fish stocking, hunting and fishing regulations, and local wildlife issues. Dottie and the other hosts helped me to relax and enjoy being behind a microphone; something I took with me for the rest of my career.

I am probably the only officer that presented a slide show on the radio. The BLM had chained [leveled with bulldozers] thousands of acres of pinion/juniper forest in Montezuma and Dolores counties. Some local people and in particular the local radio station owner Jack Hawkins were irate.

I had some colored slides that I had taken on a field trip when I was in college that demonstrated how knocking down the trees would rejuvenate the browse plants that could benefit the deer. When we were on the air, I handed Jack the slides and he described and I interpreted what he was seeing over the radio. He accepted the possibility that some good could come out of the BLM's project. I thought the broadcast went very smoothly and defused some of the emotional response in the community.

After I left the studio the dispatcher told me to drop by Scotty's house. He told me that he heard my program and that I did a good, but he handed me a folder titled "Memorandum of Understanding" (between the BLM and the Game and Fish Department). Scotty told me I didn't need to read it, but it said in effect that we stay out of their business and they stay out of ours. Then he said that the BLM owed me one for getting some folks off their backs.

I probably scared Scotty more than just that time, because previous administrations had discouraged field officers from providing news articles or contacting the media and a young upstart like me could get in over his head in controversy. Scotty never discouraged me.

My writing skills were more technical and my journalistic skills were weak, so I gave wildlife stories to the Cortez Journal news reporters, who wrote the stories. Statewide press releases have their place, but citizens in small communities like to know what is going on locally and enjoy reading about themselves and their involvement with wildlife. Small town newspapers didn't expect a local wildlife officer to be a journalist.

Soon after I started my weekly radio program I was invited to join the Cortez Toastmasters Club. I took speech in high school and college, but Toastmasters was more of a graduate level experience. Along with improving my speeches, I learned how to organize and conduct meetings. We prepared and gave speeches using the Toastmaster's workbook. Each member rotated responsibilities for critiquing grammar and evaluating each other's speeches. We learned from each other. Most of the members were businessmen and I learned so much about them and how they served their community beyond their business interests.

"I was in that class"

I got acquainted with Dave Totman, a science teacher at the Cortez High School, who reminded me of Mr. Inglis, my high school biology teacher. Both used the outdoors as a class room. I decided to help Dave just like Terrell Quick and Bob Reynolds worked with Mr. Inglis. Helping a teacher succeed would be the best way for me and the Division to educate our youth about wildlife and the environment. I gave Dave my limnology book [the study of water]and suggested some projects that his class could do at Denny Lake on the edge of town.

Migrating waterfowl made a rest stop at Denny Lake every spring and fall. I helped Dave gather binoculars and Ducks Unlimited

Canada geese on Denny Lake- Mesa Verde National Park ramparts on the horizon

waterfowl identification booklets. We took his biology class to the lake and taught them how to identify waterfowl, take that data back to their classroom and apply it to his curriculum.

Three decades later when I became the Southwest Regional Education Coordinator, I met with Brad Wayt, a Cortez elementary school principal, to schedule a teacher workshop. He asked me if I remembered taking a group of students out to Denny Lake to identify ducks. I remembered, because I only did that once. He said, "I was one of those kids."

Brad said of Mr. Totman, "We went to Denny Lake and took all kinds of water samples. We even took samples through the ice in the winter. We took them back to the classroom and he taught us how to identify and classify all the organisms. He made learning experiential and real to us. He greatly influenced me to become a teacher, because of the way he taught kids." Mr. Totman was the first teacher I ever worked with. He joined the ranks of many outstanding educators who influenced my approach to education and I worked alongside of them throughout my career.

Kids and pheasants

In the 1950s the Division and 4-H clubs developed a project for farm kids to raise pheasant chicks in those areas of Colorado where there was pheasant habitat. At that time the Cortez district had some marginal pheasant habitat. The kids not only learned how to feed and care for the birds, but the importance of wildlife habitat on the family farm. I got acquainted with parents and kids when I inspected each project.

The Division's bird farm in Rocky Ford hatched pheasant eggs and when the baby chicks were ready, the Division flew them to local communities. The kids were so excited to receive their chicks. After raising the birds all summer, I banded them and in the fall. The kids had the satisfaction of releasing the fruit of their labor.

When pheasant season opened I checked hunters who bagged a few banded birds; however, it was questionable whether the project produced many birds that survived the winters and predators. The project was cancelled when the bird farm was closed. The greatest benefit of the project was education and like most 4H projects, kids learned the rewards of being responsible stewards.

What do you do with too many deer?

Deer populations throughout Colorado were burgeoning in the late 1950s. There were too few hunters on the western slope to manage the deer population. As a result, deer and elk winter ranges were deteriorating and there were some areas where deer had starved to death for a lack of forage.

The Forest Service and BLM attended annual meetings with the Division to recommend hunting seasons and bag limits. They told us that wildlife was the State's "ball game", but they owned the "ball park" and had some legitimate concerns about deer and elk populations.

It was always a fight, because the Forest Service and BLM priorities were to graze cattle and sheep. If we reduced the deer population, that would leave more forage for cattle and sheep, but counter to the mission of the Division and the public's interest. In an effort to reduce deer populations the Wildlife Commission had established deer seasons in Montezuma and Dolores counties that extended from August to December. A late season hunt in the Disappointment Valley allowed a hunter to have three deer licenses, two of which were for does only. We shot the socks off the deer herds.

Many deer migrated from the Dolores and Mancos river drainages southward to winter ranges in Mesa Verde National Park (MVNP). Late summer range transects indicated that the resident deer had already eaten half of the current annual growth of the major browse species. The park rangers guesstimated up to 3,000 deer migrated into the park each winter. I use "guesstimate", because there was no effort to actually census the population. It was evident that the habitat couldn't sustain many more deer. Key forage plants were being over browsed. The MVNP recommended that the Division increase the harvest of migrating deer by lengthening the deer season and allowing even more doe licenses.

Jim Green U.S. Forest Service and Glen evaluating a range transect circa 1965

I recommended that they reduce the resident deer population. I didn't want to reduce the deer population that hunters could hunt outside the park.

At that time park rangers were shooting elk in Yellowstone National Park to reduce that population, so the superintendent and his staff proposed a hunting season in the MVNP to reduce the resident deer population. The public was up in arms about killing deer inside the park. The superintendent conducted a p u b l i c meeting. I had never attended a public meeting and I learned a lot from him that night. He started the meeting by holding up an overgrazed sagebrush plant and told the crowd, "This is the future of your deer herd if we don't do something. Deer have to have something to eat."

After he explained some range management principles, the audience settled down and listened. Many of the ranchers and hunters knew he was telling the truth and something did have to be done about too many deer over browsing the forage inside the park. He reached some consensus from the audience and I believe the Park would have proceeded with its proposal. As it turned out, the Department of the Interior nixed the proposal.

MVNP and Division decided to have a scientific study to determine how to manage the problem. I've observed that when the government conducts a study, the outcome usually doesn't solve the problem. A case in point began the next summer when Southwest Regional Game Biologist Errol Ryland, who had been a WCO in Durango, started a deer migration study to find out if there was a time and place outside the park boundary where hunters could harvest some of the resident deer.

We tried the newly developed capture gun technology to tranquilize some deer and tag them. Errol shot a doe with a tranquilizer dart. The deer bounded off and was picking up speed as she disappeared over a distant ridge. Errol increased the dosage for the next shot. That dart hit a deer and it dropped in its tracks. About then a tourist stopped and asked me what we were doing. I explained to him that we were tranquilizing deer just like they did on the TV show *Wild Kingdom* to study their migration and that we'd appreciate it if he would move on to reduce the stress on the deer. I didn't tell him that the deer was deader than a door nail. We gave that technique up.

Nature solved the problem in the mid 1990s when lightning caused forest fires burned large sections of Mesa Verde. The fire consumed decadent vegetation and reestablished a young ecosystem. The oak, mountain mahogany, bitter brush and other species exploded as vigorous and nutritious forage. Deer, turkey and blue grouse populations increased. With the over story burned off archeologists discovered previously unknown ruins and artifacts.

Turkey go BOOM

I cooperated with the park staff whenever they asked. I was at the headquarters when a park ranger asked me for some help to scare a pesky turkey that was messing up the building entrance. People had been feeding the bird and it knew where to get treats. I gave the ranger a cherry bomb from my tool box. The turkey was strutting near the entrance like he owned the place. The ranger lit the fuse and tossed it toward the turkey, whereupon the bird, thinking it was a treat, reached down and swallowed it. We watched in horror as the firecracker exploded, nearly decapitating the bird. A shocked ranger grabbed the carcass and ran off, leaving a trail of blood. I never knew if he ate the evidence or not. In those days there were seldom any winter visitors to witness this unexpected atrocity. Nowadays there would be a media invasion, a congressional investigation, and heads would roll.

What good is it?

A farmer called to report a strange bird that he saw in his field. I told him that he described a chukar partridge. He asked the very question that Aldo Leopold wrote about in his Sand County Almanac *". . . The last word in ignorance is the man who says of an animal or plant, 'What good is it?'"* Then he wanted to know if he could kill it. Just because at some point in time we may not understand the value of an element of nature there is no justification to destroy it. Being curious about the natural world is one thing, but deciding its value based on our economic system will leave wildlife at risk most of the time.

The chukar partridge was native to semi desert areas in the Middle East. The habitat between Cortez and Utah was good niche for the chukar. The Division had transplanted chukars in what is now The Canyons of the Ancients National Monument west of Cortez in the early 1960s. In those days biologists thought that if a project had a good chance of success; it was done without fanfare or public comment. We transplanted additional birds in 1964. The birds had survived and dispersed to surrounding habitat. In subsequent years the population has had its ups and downs; because of extended periods of deep snow is a limiting factor for chukars.

Fish management

The Cortez district had both cold and warm water fisheries. The Durango Fish Hatchery and the Dolores Rearing Unit personnel stocked catchable-sized rainbow trout in local reservoirs and streams. Like other wildlife officers, I met the fish trucks and helped the drivers unload the fish. When we had fishermen watching, I stayed around to keep the fish from being easy pickings until they could scatter. Puett and Summit reservoirs had crappie and ringed perch in addition to trout. Although the reservoirs were on private land the Division negotiated with the water users for fishermen to have public access.

The Durango Fish Hatchery put about a thousand fingerling rainbows in ten gallon milk cans that I stocked into creeks near a road. I backpacked fingerlings in oxygenated plastic bottles to the more isolated beaver dams and creeks. I wanted to improve the fishing and the only way I knew how was by stocking fish anywhere there was water. Stocking fish gave me a good feeling, but I learned that some of my efforts were a waste of time and money.

Fishermen told me stories about a monster fish in Summit Reservoir. I passed the rumor off until one evening when I checked a fisherman who had a two-pound rainbow trout with teeth marks half way up its body. Something big had tried to eat it. Dave Lemons , Southwest Regional Fish Biologist, set a gill net and caught several walleyed pike, one 32 inches long and weighing 18 pounds, which could have been the "monster". The Division had planted them several years earlier as an experiment, but considered it a failure. A few fish obviously survived. Since most fishermen fished for trout, they didn't hook into one of these lunkers. Interest in catching walleyed pike increased significantly after that.

The Montezuma Valley Irrigation Company built Totten Reservoir in 1965 just a mile east of Cortez. In cooperation with the irrigation district the Division began stocking fish. Initially we stocked rainbow trout, channel catfish, and walleyed pike. I drove up to the Hotchkiss Fish Hatchery where we netted up hundreds of bullfrogs to see if they would survive. The Division built a boat ramp and rock filled cages to provide shelter for little fish. Over the years other species such as large mouthed bass, pan fish, and northern pike have been stocked. The reservoir has become a place for bird watchers with such a variety of water birds and other species to congregate. The area is now the Totten State Wildlife Area administered by the Division of Parks and Wildlife.

CHAPTER 6
When horses and mules wear diamonds

Even though I grew up in the city, I had a fascination with horses. Roy Rogers, Gene Autry, and the Lone Ranger were my radio and movie heroes as well as their horses Trigger, Champion, and Silver. I knew that mountain game wardens rode horses and that I should learn how to ride. In my freshman year at CSU I signed up for a horsemanship course. An old cowboy taught the class how to ride, feed, and care for horses. It was a good introduction, but I had many more skills to learn.

Since the Cortez district had a maze of back country roads, I didn't need a horse. Scotty decided to expand my experience and that I should learn how to ride and pack horses. I was a willing student. Scotty asked, Gene Bassett, the officer in Bayfield, to take me on one of his pack trips into what is now the Weminuche Wilderness Area. [The wilderness area was named for the Weminuche band of the Ute Indian tribe.]

Gene asked Scotty, "What horse should I have him ride?" Scotty answered, "Give him that new one that's never been ridden and let them learn together." Gene was an old cowboy and he knew horses, packing, and people. I knew that I was in the hands of a master, but what I didn't know was that if a coyote were riding with Gene, it would starve to death. His priority was working-not eating.

The day came when I drove to Bayfield and met Gene and his wife Joan. We loaded Gene's horses and mules and drove to the Pine River trailhead on the northern shore of Vallecito Reservoir. We were going to set up a base camp at Rock Lake for Gene to use while patrolling a wilderness early buck season.

Gene taught me how to tie the double-diamond hitch to secure the panniers on his pack horses and mules. Although there are other hitches, the double diamond was the only hitch I ever used. We rode up the Pine River trail into one of the most beautiful wilderness areas in the Rockies. The river plunged over waterfalls, cascaded down rapids and meandered through mountain meadows with crystal clear pools. Native cutthroat trout darted after insects floating with the current. There are so many scenes like this in the Colorado Rockies.

We checked a few fishermen along the river. After a nineteen mile ride, we arrived at the Granite Peaks Guard Station, a Forest Service cabin used by summer work crews. The next day we would complete our ride to Rock Lake. We unloaded the pack animals, and turned them into a pasture, and stowed our gear in the cabin. We had skipped lunch and it never occurred to me to bring some snacks with me. It was evening when Gene said, "Let's go look for some more fishermen." My aching body didn't want to go and I was hungry, but I was raised to obey my elders. We rode off to search for more fishermen.

We saw smoke rising from a campfire up ahead. Gene reined up and said, "Follow my lead." I pondered "What does that mean?" He spurred his horse and my mount decided he had to gallop too. I hung on for dear life as the wide-eyed dudes watched us gallop into their camp. Gene's horse reared up and he stepped off, just like Roy Rogers, tipped his hat and calmly asked, "How you folks doing?" My horse came to a screeching halt and I uncowboy-like slipped off the saddle, unnoticed by the wide-eyed dudes I'm sure.

We checked some cutthroats being prepared for supper. I couldn't believe it when Gene turned down the offer for supper and a place to spend the night. Gene said, "Naw, we gotta ride on and we'll sleep under a big spruce tonight." Those dudes must have thought we were the two tough toughest hombres on the mountain. Instead, we rode back to the cabin for the night. Gene did warm up a can of spaghetti for supper. We laid our sleeping bags on soft mattresses. I quickly went to sleep with echoes of the beauty and experiences of the day. I loved it.

The next day we arose before dawn. Gene's rule was, "We can't be burning daylight." It was important to get an early start to avoid being exposed above timberline in the afternoon when the lightning in thunderstorms can be fatal. I was so stiff and sore. We probably had some breakfast. We packed up again. I had learned my role in packing a horse. I stood on one side of the horse and Gene on the other and followed his instructions to the letter. He taught me that it was most important to balance the pack. If a pack does start to shift to one side or the other, Gene just put a rock on the lite side.

We were soon on the trail up Rincon La Osa Creek [the Valley of the Bear]] This whole area had been a grizzly bear refuge from 1955 through the early 1965 and was thought to be the last home of the great bear.

However, in 1979 a grizzly attacked Ed Wiseman in the South San Juan Wilderness near Platoro, Colorado. Lloyd Anderson, a federal trapper, had killed a grizzly bear in the Pine River drainage in 1952 and he had reported seeing grizzlies as late as 1967. The thought of riding upon the great bear crossed my mind and had me watching.

I felt the humbling isolation that comes from being beyond civilization; just like I had experienced hiking with my dad. In addition to those nostalgic feelings, I looked at the wilderness differently now. I had the new responsibility of being a caretaker and steward of these wild places. After a long ride we topped out above timberline on the Continental Divide Trail on Sawtooth Ridge. I looked below at Ute Lake, but instead of the anticipation of catching fish, I now looked at the lake in terms of what species of fish were there and their condition. There were no fishermen, and I hadn't packed my fishing rod.

Sitting on my horse at over 12,000 feet, I was overwhelmed by awesome panorama of the Ute Creek Basin and on the horizon were peaks named Nebo, Leviathan, Silex, the Guardian, Silex, and Storm

King, Weminuche, and other peaks all stretched their pinnacles more than 13,000 feet into the

The Continental Divide Trail at Sawtooth Ridge, Weminuche Wilderness circa 1966

sky. The scene created echoes that still thrill my soul and is the cover photo of this book. George Catlin, an early 19th century traveler, called these mountains *"soul intoxicating scenery."* Little did I know that in another year the scene below me would be in my district.

We rode past Flint Lake and camped for the night at timberline near Rock Lake. We pitched tents, gathered firewood, and fed the horses. Gene warmed up another can of something over the campfire. The experiences of that day transcended the pain of my saddle sores. This was the life for me.

After dark we laid next to the campfire and Gene mesmerized me with his stories of adventures in the San Juans. I couldn't help but think that someday I would make memories and share my own wilderness adventures. Maybe I'd even take a trainee on his first pack trip and pass on what I was learning from Gene

The third day on the trail was downright painful. Although Gene's horses were not trotters we trotted twenty-six miles down Vallecito Creek. A million times the saddle came up as my body came down, meeting at the old saddle horn. Real cowboys don't cry because of pain - they yodel! I suppressed my yodeling, so I wouldn't scare the horses. Vallecito Creek was just as beautiful as the Pine River, but in every direction I looked it was straight up at towering peaks. We ended our ride at the Wits End Ranch.

The rancher had relayed Gene's truck and trailer to the ranch. They invited us in for lunch. Finally, real food! What impressed me more than the hospitality and food was the close relationship Gene had with our hosts. They shared a friendship beyond respect. Gene had that skill of "getting along with people." My saddle sores lasted only a few days, but the memories of that ride with Gene will last until the day I die. Gene Bassett will always be a legend to everyone who had the privilege of riding with him. He taught me about horses, mules and the double-diamond hitch.

Division personnel had neck banded elk in the Animas Valley above Durango in the winter to study their migration and to learn where they spent the summer. We often flew aerial searches, but that technique isn't effective in heavily timbered mountains. I went on a pack trip with WCOs Allison Mason, Wayne Knisley and Regional Biologist Errol Ryland up Hermosa Creek to look for banded elk on the divide between the Dolores and Animas Rivers.

After we set up base camp we paired off to look for elk. I was bushwhacking on game trails with Allison through some heavy timber and I had no idea where we were. I asked Allison, "You ever been here before?" He answered, "Next time will make twice." We searched for several days and saw lots of elk, but no banded ones.

Technology has advanced to such an extent that ground searches are seldom used anymore. Animals are now trapped and fitted with GPS transmitters. A biologist can sit in an office with a computer and track in real time the location of an animal. Other features may include a mortality signal. If an animal doesn't move within twelve hours, the radio signal changes and a biologist can use GPS coordinates and go immediately to the site, necropsy the animal to determine cause of death or gather any other data that adds to our knowledge of wildlife.

Getting out into the field however, had value beyond just locating banded elk. Allison taught me about wildlife history, range management. and the geology of the San Juans. He was a fountain of information and an historian with remarkable insight. His dry sense of humor always lifted the spirit. He came into camp carrying a rock and said it was a fine a specimen of Leaverite. "Probably will run 2,000 pounds to the ton, as he threw it on the ground and explained, "'Leaver right' there, because it is worthless." Allison was also an experienced horseman and packer I was proud of myself, having learned from Gene Bassett how to tie the double- diamond hitch and could be of more help on the trip. Pack trips are different when you are working, compared to if you are recreating. Still, I lived to be high in the mountains, working or playing made little difference.

CHAPTER 7
My dream district

Beth and I had been in Cortez two years when our daughter Lois was born. Thirteen months later Ralph was born. Life was good and stable. The Division had a policy that new officers would be transferred every three years so they could experience mountain, prairie, and metropolitan districts. The diverse experiences were intended to prepare an officer to climb the agency ladder. One of the problems with the policy was that there wasn't room at the top for everyone. Many officers like me wanted to be career district officers and I wanted mountains - lots of mountains.

In the summer of 1966 I got word that I was going to be transferred, but another possibility opened up for me when Jesse Williams, the Southwest Regional Information and Education (I & E) Specialist resigned and became the New Mexico Game and Fish Department I & E Chief.

I had demonstrated a deep seated and proven interest in I & E. A degree in journalism was not required and I applied for the job. I scored high enough on the test that I would have been offered the position, but Director Woodward decided not to fill the position at that time. I'm glad the Lord closed that door and opened a new one.

The Continental Divide at Stony Pass, elevation 12,650 ft. above sea level. The Rio Grande River headwaters begin here on its 1,900 mile journey to the Gulf of Mexico

I always wanted a mountain district and boy did I ever get a mountain district. The Creede district was open and Scotty thought it was the kind of district I would do well in. Even though the Cortez district was considered a mountain district, Scotty and Regional Manager Smoky Till influenced the decision to transfer me to Creede.

I had mixed feelings about leaving Cortez. It takes about three yearsto learn the topography and resources o f a district and it takes longer to get acquainted with people and gain their

The Rio Grande begins from snow melt, tiny springs, and gathers tributaries into a mighty river.

confidence and trust. I hadn't been there long enough to give back to the community. But, it was time to move on.

The Continental Divide enfolds the headwaters of the Rio Grande River, beginning at Stony Pass at 12,650 feet above sea level. There are five hundred miles of streams on forty-seven drainages, fifty-five lakes and reservoirs (public and private) in about eight hundred square miles. (If you flattened it out it would more than double that size.) In 1966 portions of the Upper Rio Grande had not yet been mapped by the U.S. Geological Survey. The forests were aspen and spruce/fir and above timberline the alpine tundra. Big game winter range was grass, aspen, and willows and there were no major browse species. Much of the area was wilderness and roadless. There were only seven miles of paved highway in the district from Wagonwheel Gap to Creede. Only five per cent of the district was private land, so I didn't have any game damage problems.

ranchers grazed cattle in the summer and transported them to market or to winter pastures in the San Luis Valley.

The Rio Grande flows through the San Luis Valley, which I will refer to through the rest of this book as the Valley. The Valley floor is a flat 122 miles long and 75 miles wide at an average elevation of about 7,500 feet above sea level. It is bounded on the west by the San Juan Mountains and on the east by the Sangre de Cristo Mountains. Alamosa is the largest city in the Valley and often has the nation's lowest temperature during the winter months

The Valley is an agriculture area producing potatoes, wheat, barely, lettuce, cattle, and sheep. The Rio Grande and artesian wells irrigate crop lands and sustains wetlands and some lakes for recreational purposes. Hispanic settlers from New Mexico established the town of San Luis in 1851, making it the oldest town in Colorado. The Valley is home of the Great Sand Dunes National Park and Adams State University. Although six wildlife officers had their own district responsibilities, we worked together as if there were no boundaries.

It's Day All Day in the Daytime

Scotty arranged for Wayne Russell to fly me over the Creede District to give me an idea of what the country looked like. Even though there were portions of San Juan, Hinsdale and Mineral counties, Creede, population 350, was the only town in the district. Portions of the three counties combined made it one of the least

Creede Colorado looking toward Wagonwheel Gap.

populated areas in Colorado.

Creede was the last silver boom towns in Colorado.   Silver was discovered in 1889 and in its heyday it grew to over 10,000 people until the Silver Panic of 1893. In 1892 Cy Warman, editor of the Creede Chronicle wrote, *"It's day all day in the day time and there is no night in C r e e d e ."* Creede had a reputation of being a   pretty wild town, but it was tamed down by the time I got there.

A few days after my flight Beth and I checked the town out. We noted the log school buildings, a block long business district, some houses looked abandoned, others boarded up for the winter, and frankly the town didn't seem like a place to raise a family. Beth remarked about being able to see through a house with front and back doors closed. The town appeared abandoned as the tourist businesses were already closed for the winter. We didn't see any people on the streets. I wondered how Beth was going to feel about raising two babies in the outback. I could put in for a transfer, but we stayed for nearly twenty-two years.

We didn't know where we were going to live. The housing situation was solved when Don Benson, the Area Supervisor for the Valley, arranged for us to live in the superintendent's house at the abandoned Creede Federal Fish Hatchery on the banks of the Rio Grande about two miles from town. The federal government transferred the property to the Division with the caveat that the property would be used for wildlife conservation purposes. The state had no interest in operating the hatchery, because it was not economical.

Since the house wasn't ready to live in, Don arranged for us to stay in one of the Wason Ranch cabins until we could make the house livable. Rod and Marilyn Wintz managed the ranch and we became good friends. The log cabins were not winterized.   There was cold running water, a hot plate, and a wood burning cook stove for heat. It was late October and the temperature dropped below freezing every night

First impressions

That first night I stood outside our cabin taking in the crisp mountain air and the Milky Way seemed so close. I was feeling the humbling emotion stimulated by my new district, when across the valley on Snowshoe Mountain, I saw some vehicle headlights coming down a jeep road. Hunting season was still open, but it was dark and past legal hunting hours. The vehicle brake lights came on and the driver flashed his headlights up into the edge of the timber. It looked like he was using his headlights to spotlight elk or deer. I drove to where he came onto the Deep Creek road and stopped the truck.

I told the driver that I had been watching him use his headlights. He said, "I thought I might catch one coming out of the timber." I told him that I was glad he didn't "catch" one, because I just caught him. He asked, "Who are you?" I introduced myself as the new wildlife officer in Creede. I told him I really wanted to get along with folks and I'd appreciate it if he would come off the mountain a little earlier. He seemed agreeable.

The next morning I drove into Creede to Ivan Weaver's drug store, the local coffee spot. All eyes were on me as I walked in to start meeting the Creede folks. I introduced myself, but they already knew who I was, where I had come from, and the worst of my reputation from Cortez which had preceded me.

Over a cup of coffee, Bud Ames asked, "What kind of a game warden are you going to be?" I answered, "That depends mostly on you folks. If people are violating the wildlife laws then I will probably be writing tickets. On the other hand, if people obey the laws, then together we can take care of the fish and game and even improve the hunting and fishing."

I sought the counsel of my predecessor Billy Shultz, who retired in Creede after being the wildlife officer in the district for the previous twenty years. His advise to me: "Tear page thirteen out of your law book and then you can't go by the book all the time; just substitute good judgment." Billy shared valuable

Beth, Ralph, Lois and Glen at home with the Rio Grande in our backyard Circa 1967

history from a wildlife officer's perspective that gave me insight to understand this tight knit community, but he didn't tell me how to run the district.

The Rio Grande reminded me so much of the Colorado River in Middle Park. I knew what good river fishing was like: wild jumping, fighting rainbows and deep running brown trout. I had experienced fantastic high country lake fishing and superb reservoir fishing. I was not a rookie officer and I had learned in Cortez that it took more than law enforcement to manage wildlife. Bud Hurd's advice rang true, "Get along with people."

Gene McClure, one of the town patriarchs, asked me how I felt about feeding elk. I told him that in my opinion feeding elk and deer wasn't a good idea except during the worst possible winters. I didn't know it, but that was the answer he wanted to hear. In the harsh winter of 1964 there was a confrontation between Creede people and the Division about feeding elk. The Creede people fed the elk to the objection of the Division. There were lingering hard feelings and mistrust. I soon learned about the awesome independence of Creede and became a part of its culture. It was fruitless for governmental agencies to tell Creede people they couldn't do something. They were people who greatly cared for each other and the wildlife of the Upper Rio Grande.

Gene and his wife Bea owned Tomkins Hardware. He told m e to come to the store and talk about our furnace. Gene said a little girl suffered severe burns when she fell onto the hot furnace grate. He didn't want to see that happen again. We fabricated a two foot high expanded metal fence around the grate. I hadn't been in town but a day and I learned that they cared for one another and even my family whom they didn't know.

Preparing our nest

The Creede Federal Fish Hatchery was closed by the U.S. Fish and Wildlife Service in 1964, because it had become uneconomical. The hatchery superintendent's house was built in 1930 and it had been vacant for two years. When Horace Wheeler, a retired miner and our neighbor across the river, learned we were going to live there, he came over and removed the wooden shutters from the windows before we arrived. "Ish" steward, Creede's handyman, got the water pump working. The house walls were not insulated. A coal and wood burning floor furnace in the center of the house was the only heat source.

Our house was not unique. The majority of houses in Creede were heated with wood and coal at that time. We bought coal from Tomkins Hardware. Firewood was free for the cutting and taking off the national forest. I cut, split, and stacked about ten cords of firewood and put two tons of coal in the coal bin. It took me awhile to learn how much fuel and air flow it took to keep the house warm when temperatures plunged to thirty or forty below zero. I emptied ashes every day during the winter. We kept a trickle of water running all winter to prevent water from freezing even though the water pipe from the well to the house was buried eight feet deep. The glazing on the single-paned windows had dried and cracked allowing the cold wind into the house. I glazed glass panes, caulked window frame edges, and placed plastic sheeting over all the windows to keep the wind out.

I had one unusual adventure gathering firewood which answered the question, "Does a tree falling in the forest make a noise?" I learned it makes very loud noise, especially when it falls on your truck. I felled a tree for firewood, but it fell 180 degrees in the wrong direction. At the next inservice school, I was given "The Most Unusual Accident of the Year" award.

Beth had the biggest job of preparing our nest.

"When I walked in the front door of this wonderfully big house and saw the beautiful built in library that divided the living room from the dining room and built in hutch, I knew I was going to love living here. With the house having been vacant for two years the place was filthy. I kept Lois and Ralph in a play pen until I got the floors swept and mopped and the house vacuumed. The cold floors had no rugs."

After Beth painted the kitchen, we had our furniture moved and set up housekeeping. With two babies in diapers Beth did a lot of laundry. Paper diapers hadn't been invented yet. She hung the laundry outside on the clothes lines. It was a l r e a d y so cold that the laundry froze on the lines. After we got the metal fence around the furnace grate it made a great place to dry diapers. It didn't take us long however, to buy an electric clothes dryer and a rug for the living room.

Women who moved to high altitude learned to adjust their cooking recipes. Beth said, "I had to   change recipes for such things as bread,   cakes,   and cinnamon rolls.   A *Good Housekeeping Cook Book* w a s of some help."

I was concerned that being two miles from town, the wife of a law enforcement officer, and being new to a little town would have caused Beth to feel socially isolated.   Beth's attitude was, "This was a n e w adventure that the Lord had for us and I was going to enjoy it. Having grown up on a farm I was more used to inconveniences and distance from shopping.

Beth hanging laundry on a cold winter day

There were no large stores, but we had Wards, Sears, and Penneys catalogues. You just got used to traveling fifty miles to the doctor or dentist. We bought locally when we could. I gradually got acquainted and fell in love with the Creede people and the mountains."

Beth was a skilled seamstress sewing clothes, down insulated sleeping bags, and parkas and one year she made cheerleader uniforms for the high school girls pep squad. She enjoyed being a substitute teacher. Beth also learned how to regulate the furnace Belching Bertha so named for its tendency to build up unburned gases until it went "POOF" and blew dust all over the house. It w a s a constant chore keeping the house clean, but we soon adapted to our new home. When I was gone on assignments, she kept the home fire burning.

Getting to know the land and people

While Beth was making the house livable, I still had to work the remainder of the hunting season. Toward the end of the season however, there were only a few hunters in the district. It hadn't snowed yet so I was able to drive around to learn some of the country. State highway 149 was paved from South Fork to Creede, but the fifty-two miles to Lake City was gravel until 1983 when it was paved and kept open year around. During the winter months the highway was plowed for twenty miles and snowbound beyond. Someone said that Creede wasn't the end of the world, but you could see it from there with a good pair of binoculars.

I felt like I was driving to the end of the world on my first venture toward the headwaters of the Rio Grande. A rancher was stretching fence next to the road, so I stopped and introduced myself to Charlie Kipp and offered to help. Over the years I learned a lot from Charlie. As with several other outfitters, he showed me the trails and shortcuts where he provided guide service. He and his wife Hilda owned the Wetherill Ranch [RC Guest Ranch], once owned by the descendants of the famous Wetherill family who discovered the ruins in Mesa Verde National Park.

Beyond Rio Grande Reservoir the small creeks had already built up ice across the road. I hadn't seen anyone for miles and stopped, because if I slid off the road or got stuck, I was forty miles up river, beyond radio contact and nobody knew where I was. Further exploration would have to wait until next summer.

My other calling

After we had been in Creede a short time Beth started teaching a Sunday school class, but after a while the minister decided he didn't want us teaching Sunday school any longer. After discussing the issue with parents we started a Sunday school in our house. We soon had a houseful of kids coming to learn about Jesus. Some teenagers got interested in a Bible study and before long, adults began coming for Bible study and worship. We had no denominational affiliation.

Some small town churches have difficulty retaining pastors. When a pastor left, I sometimes filled pulpits in the Community and Baptist churches. Sundays were always busy for me, but in the absence of a pastor I filled pulpits and Beth and I taught Sunday school. I went out early to check fishermen, came back to town, changed out of my uniform in time to deliver the morning sermon. I surprised more than one fisherman whom I had checked fishing earlier in the morning and when he came to church found me preaching.

To me Christianity is not a stereotype lifestyle of following a set of rules, taboos, ethics, legalisms, and nostalgic traditions. Rather, God created us to have a relationship with Himself. I believe that Jesus Christ died for our sins. Out of that relationship He ministers to people that He brings into our lives. Our role is to love and serve one another. I tried to see fishermen, hunters, miners, visitors, and townspeople, lost and hurt folks as those who crossed my "trail" and whom God brought into my life. When I caught a poacher, I thought that just maybe, God wanted him caught. God is glorified by what He does in our lives, more than what we think we do for Him. This has been my experience. I'm not perfect or holier t h a n any one. People who have known me know that for a fact.

Beth and I had opportunity to serve the Creede community in many ways. Living in Creede was exciting. We felt at home and comfortable in Creede, a community of people who cared for each other and sacrificed time, money, and efforts for the betterment of all. Creede was a wonderful place to live and raise our family. I will always consider Creede as my hometown and the Upper Rio Grande as my district.

Creede Colorado
Main Street business district has had the
same appearance for many decades.
Businesses and paint colors have changed,
but the same spirit of community continues.

Photo by Mike
Warrick

CHAPTER 8
I love small town life

You know a town is small when Second Street is the edge of town. Creede was a close knit community. Several generations of families have lived there since the 1890s. Families were often related or very close to one another. The mines were producing tons of silver, lead, and zinc. The Rio Grande Railroad hauled gondolas loaded with concentrated ore twice a week to a smelter in El Paso, Texas. The population of 350 residents increased to over 1,000 when the Homestake and other mines opened in the early 1970s.

Creede functioned like many isolated small towns. A box labeled CREEDE was on the counter at the Adams Drug Store forty-two miles away in Del Norte. The druggist placed prescriptions for Creede residents in the box and anyone coming through picked up the medicines and took them to the Creede Standard Station. Folks picked up their medications or when someone was really sick, the prescription was personally delivered.

Everyone picked their mail up at the post office and it was the center for "community information" while people waited for the mail to be put up. I placed a bulletin board in the post office on which I posted a weekly wildlife story. It gave people something to read besides wanted posters.

I was posting an article one day when Steve O'Rourke, the new owner of the Mineral County Miner and South Fork Tine newspaper, asked me to write a column for his paper. I took my bulletin board down and started writing for the paper. This gave me the opportunity to communicate with the local people and summer residents. Steve edited my articles, which improved them. I wrote my weekly Warden's Corner column for twenty years. I also listed wildlife citations in the Wildlife Blotter, which was a small deterrent to some violators lest they get their name in the paper.

I had only been in Creede a couple years when the Southwest Regional I&E position opened again. Beth and I decided that I was gone from home enough and that it was having an adverse effect on our children, so I didn't apply. It was a position that would require more travel and time away from my family. My interest and experience in I & E however, intensified throughout my career.

When my former supervisor Harvey Bray accepted the position as the Director of the Tennessee Wildlife Resource Agency, he asked me to go with him to head it's I & E Section. I felt honored, but I didn't want to leave the mountains of Colorado and I didn't feel I had the technical or administrative experience to step into such a role.

When I first got to Creede I contacted a few fishermen who were violating some minor regulations. I could tell that they didn't know the law and those license agents, resort operators, and others had given them outdated information. It was easy to lecture people to be responsible for reading and following the regulations and give them a ticket to enforce the law. I decided on a better long term approach in a small community would be more successful.

I asked members of the Upper Rio Grande Fish and Game Association to help me with this problem. It was to their advantage as well as their guests to work together. As a result, I wrote a "Welcome to the Upper Rio Grande" letter explaining some of the fishing regulations that people were having a problem with. Resort owners posted the letter on the doors of their cabins and rooms. The Forest Service posted the letter in their campgrounds.

The letter must have helped, because the violation rate went down for those minor violations. The Association printed and posted posters that said, "Report Wildlife Violators Here" and bright orange bumper stickers that said, "God's Wildlife Belongs to all - don't waste it." Because so many Valley people hunted and fished in the Upper Rio Grande, I tape recorded radio programs for radio station KSLV in Monte Vista and wrote press releases for other Valley newspapers. For several years Tom Rauch, the wildlife officer in Monte Vista had a weekly radio program as well.

When I was on patrol I made a point to stop at resorts, ranches, and license agents. I delivered the fishing and hunting regulations. These people were my eyes and ears. Wildlife officers learn where to stop for coffee and to break bread. For instance, when I checked the fishermen at Brown Lakes State Wildlife Area and Black Mountain Lake, I went on over to the Pearl Lakes Trout Club. Thursday was an especially good day to get the latest observations from caretaker Barney Fairchild. It also just happened to be the day of the week that Arletta's famous cinnamon rolls were floating out of her oven. A wildlife officer's nose homes in on fresh cinnamon rolls, like a bear to honey. Some ranches, resorts, and trout clubs owned private lakes, which they licensed with the state. They stocked their own fish and controlled the catch. Guests or members could fish without licenses and the owner issued a permit for them to possess and transport the fish. A few people tried to leave without permits or with more fish than were allowed. When this happened I got a call and stopped the suspect. If there was a violation, I wrote a citation and reported the violator to the appropriate owner.

It takes time to develop trust. I contacted a man when I was in the Cortez district who told me, "You will never catch me poaching." I took that as a challenge until he explained that if he were caught poaching it would break Harry Terrell's (my predecessor) heart. They had been friends for many years. He so respected Harry, earned his trust, and he wouldn't do anything to endanger that friendship. Trusting people is risky, but people who violate a trust are the losers.

I experienced this when I caught a friend in a willful violation. I wrote him a ticket. A couple days later he came to me and apologized for violating the law and he felt badly for having violated my trust. He asked me to forgive him. Without hesitation I extended my hand and assured him that I didn't take things personally and I would always consider him a good friend. In my eyes, he fully restored his integrity. It takes a real man to admit wrong doing and humbly ask forgiveness. My forgiving him released me from being judgmental toward him. A friendship is too precious to discard when one seeks to restore a strained relationship.

Hunters, chili, and the prom

Small mountain towns enthusiastically welcomed deer and elk hunters. Fluorescent orange hats and vests were standard garb and as many as 4,000 hunters from all over the United States came to the Upper Rio Grande. For many businesses the deer and elk seasons were the last economic boost that got them through the winter.

Someone came up with the idea of having a hunter's night before the opening of the deer and elk season. The high school junior class sponsored the event in the school gymnasium. Local hunters donated elk meat and volunteers prepared gourmet elk chili. The class sold delicious homemade pies and pastries that visiting hunters relished. Local merchants donated door prizes and a rifle was raffled. Visiting hunters and local folks enjoyed breaking bread together. The Forest Service presented travel management maps and other information. I gave a presentation about the latest hunting regulations and any other hunting information.

The main event however, was the evening program. One of the most memorable programs was the night that I invited Larry

Helberg, Colorado State Forest Entomologist, and his alter ego.

The Rattlesnake came screaming like a bearded banshee into the school gymnasium. Wearing buckskins, coonskin cap, carrying his pack and his trusty muzzleloader *Wart*, Larry had the children running to their parents and everyone was taken back by this brash mountain man out of the 1800s.

The Rattlesnake mesmerized the crowd with his tales of the hunting in his day. He poked fun at our modern rifles and hunting paraphernalia. He talked about the ethics of a mountain man and his relationship to the natural world. Larry not only entertained his audience, but subtly reminded hunters of their responsibility toward wildlife, the land, and each other. It was a fun evening.

The next morning *The Rattlesnake* presented an assembly about early day trapping and conservation to the Creede Elementary School children. Education best takes place with "teachable moments". The annual chili supper provided that opportunity. For several years hunters planned their hunting trips to come a couple days early just so they could attend the annual chili supper and program. The junior class often made enough profit to pay for the junior-senior prom the following spring.

I took advantage of teachable moments whenever possible. I lived trapped a beaver and took it to the elementary school so kids could have a "hands on" experience" of seeing, but not actually touching an animal. I ordered a Division movie on the life of a beaver for the teacher to follow up on the opportunity.

I was a guest speaker for many classes over the years. When a science teacher got sick in such a small school district, the principal called upon citizens to substitute. I substituted for science teachers.

Bachelor Survival 101

Charlene Quiller Ameel was the Creede High School home economics teacher who started a bachelor survival course for boys. Her curricula included everything from writing a check to cooking and taking care of themselves. I got my hands on an illegal deer and asked Charlene if she wanted to use the deer for a teaching opportunity. She thought that since most of the boys were hunters, it was a good idea to teach them how to care for and cook wild came. I brought the skinned carcass into the home economics room. Along with my knives and other supplies. I got some wild game recipe books from the CSU Extension Service. and

Glen and Charlene review lesson plans Photo by Geoff Tischbein

demonstrated how to sharpen knives and safely use them. The boys learned where the various cuts of meat came from and proceeded to butcher the deer. As part of their curriculum the boys prepared a delicious venison dinner for the senior citizens.

Glen, Mike Kolisch, Dwight Miller, Kirk Ellison, David Mallow butcher a deer in class
Photo by Geoff Tischbein

Bring your guns to school

Hunter safety was within the school physical education curriculum. When I taught during the school day, I couldn't take the kids out of town to shoot their guns. Leonard "Gus" Gustafson, a local carpenter, built a bullet backstop on the school playground. After the classroom instruction and testing were finished, I told the kids to bring their .22 rifles to school (with parental permission) and leave them in the principal's office. They brought their unloaded guns with actions open for inspection. When it came time to shoot the kids, I took them onto the playground and had each of them shoot ten rounds and demonstrate safe gun handling.

When I started teaching the course after school hours, I had parents bring Their kids and .22s outside of town. I demonstrated the destructive power of differentkinds of firearms. I used a movie, *"ThisLittle Bullet"*, featuring John Wayne. The "Duke" himself introduced

Glen oversees a young marksman

sharpshooters who demonstrated the awesome damage little bullets are capable of inflicting. It was just a movie, but I wanted to impress upon parents and kids that firearms are not toys and that they have a responsibility for the firearm safety in their homes.

Then, the kids got to shoot their ten rounds. Over the years the Division has invested time and money to train volunteer hunter education instructors. While I was in Creede, Kelly Mortenson was my volunteer instructor. Kelly taught hundreds of hunters and I just helped him. In all my years in the Creede district we did not have a single gunshot fatality and only a couple gun related accidents.

Scouting adventures

Harry Larson, the Mineral County Sheriff, invited me to go to a Boy Scout meeting in Monte Vista. He had a passion for the boys in town. I had no idea what I was getting myself into. On the way home he asked me to be the Boy Scout Master for the Creede troop. I had been a Cub Scout, but because my dad often took me fishing and camping, I never joined the Boy Scouts. I accepted the role and began an adventure with a fine bunch of boys. Boy Scouts is far more than camping and woodsmanship.

We conducted our scout meetings in the upstairs workshop at the Creede hatchery. In the winter we built a fire in a potbellied stove. It was a challenge to keep the room warm enough, but the boys worked on their merit badges and we had fun. Some of the dads wanted to help, but miners worked rotating shifts, making it difficult for them to fit into our weekly scout meetings. In the summer I took the boys camping and taught woodsmanship, and we played a lot of games. I was just a few years older than the oldest boys and was able to keep up with them. I learned that the secret to staying young was to associate with young people, but trying to keep up with them can cause premature aging.

Schedule-wise I had the same problem that miners had. I was on twenty-four hour call seven days a week. My job responsibilities were a higher priority than my role of a Scout Master. With no assistant scout master I had to cancel some activities that disappointed the boys. The last straw came when we were ready for a camping trip and I got called out on a search and rescue mission just a few hours before we were to leave. I had to cancel the trip. The troop folded. I still fondly remember my boys and am proud of them becoming good men.

Another world

I've always lived on the mountains. It wasn't until I moved to Creede that I was introduced to the world under them. I listened to miners talk about drifts, raises, stopes, muck, and descriptions of their underground world that I could only imagine. The only things I knew about mining were on the surface such as a mill and tailing ponds.

The Homestake Mining Company invited me and others to see a water problem in the mine. Water seeped through the mountain which had to be pumped out of the mine or else that part of the mine would flood. The company wanted us to understand that it was going to be necessary to pump some muddy water   out of the mine that would flow down Willow Creek and into the Rio Grande. The flow would be brief, nontoxic, and would cause less turbidity in the river than runoff from a rainstorm. I saw no problem with their plan and was anxious to go on the tour.

After we listened to a mine safety lecture, we donned boots, raincoats, battery packs, headlamps, and helmets. We boarded the train, ducked low, and followed the main drift [tunnel] more than a mile into the mountain. The mountain's ambient temperature was a cool fifty-two degrees. Huge fans piped fresh air to all parts of the mine. We arrived at a raise (vertical shaft) and took an elevator to the bottom of the mine. We walked along a drift and entered a cavern like stope. Right in front of us was a sloping vein of high grade silver ore sparkling in our lights. I then understood the beauty these men saw in their work. It was a fascinating world. Miners stood on scaffolding and pressed their jack-leg drills into the rock face where they would soon insert explosives. Hard rock miners are strong men working in a dangerous environment. Safety was on everyone's mind.

I came out of that mine with a respect greater for those men than any of them ever knew. Our computers and high tech gizmos wouldn't function without silver and it is the miner who extracts this precious metal from the mountains.

Just like those of us who were trained to understand, respect, and work in an outdoor environment, miners understood and respected the mountain. They lived or died by mountain rules, as well as all the regulations imposed upon the industry. I felt safe when I was underground, but I must admit I wasn't comfortable there. I value the experiences of that day. I understood a little more why a small mining town is so closely knit. These men could depend on each other for their very lives. Every miner I ever knew loved his work and when he came out of the mine he enjoyed the out-of-doors. They respected the wildlife and wild places as much or more than anyone.

CHAPTER 9
Miscellaneous duties as assigned

Colorado Wildlife officers are generalists who handle most biological, law enforcement and public relations responsibilities in a district. Some opportunities were assigned and others were taken on as a personal initiative. We brought different backgrounds and talents to the job and complimented one another. The Division took advantage of our strengths by giving us the independence to use them such as my bend toward I & E. The official job description ended with "and other duties as assigned" category that added a lot of diversity to an already interesting job. It all paid the same. In the 1970s the Division began hiring more specialized terrestrial and aquatic biologists and wildlife property technicians to help carry the ever increasing work load.

The biggest change came when the Department of Labor sued the Division in 1986 because we were working too many hours even though we were salaried. We reported hours worked and like most officers I averaged well over two-hundred hours a month [165 hours is the average month for a forty-hour week] and during hunting seasons nearly three-hundred hours in a month was not unusual.

We worked those long hours, weekends, and holidays without compensatory pay or time off and there was no complaining. Being able to take my family with me at times and having job independence were compensation enough. When the trainee program started in 1971 new recruits worked month long assignments without days off so they would get used to the long hours.

The Fair Labor Standards Act was decreed in 1989 and was one of the most demoralizing actions taken against us, especially during hunting season. We had to change the way we worked by planning days off, spending less time contacting businesses, license agents, ranchers, resorts, and being in the public eye. We scheduled our time so that an officer in the Valley was always on call. The public started complaining that they didn't see us as much. We had to concentrate more on violators who were causing significant damage the wildlife resource and that meant being less visible to the public.

Counting elk

One of the exciting jobs I had was making the fall and winter elk sex ratio counts. I went on my first elk count sitting between pilot Virgil Jones and biologist Ray Boyd. Virgil revved up the Bell-47 and as we lifted off, my harness pulled me back against the seat. I felt like I was going to fall forward out into space. The noise was so loud that we had to yell at each other and Ray directed Virgil with hand signals. Virgil approached a herd to spread it out like a deck of cards so Ray could classify them. Ray talked into his tape recorder "Cow, calf, spike, bull. . ." He taught me how to tell the difference between cows and calves from the air. We made no attempt to count all the elk, but recorded a sample of about 2,000 elk in the Upper Rio Grande. We used this data along with a winter count and harvest data to determine herd size and calf production. That information along with other observations were the basis for our recommendations to the Wildlife Commission for season structure and license numbers. My first flight was so exciting that I ceased being afraid almost immediately.

Chopper closes in on a herd of elk on Long Ridge

Whether you're counting elk, deer, or bighorn sheep; from a chopper there is no room for pilot error. Choppers have the aerodynamics of a round rock. If the engine or any significant system fails (they are all significant) you are going to crash. Counting elk was an adrenaline rush, but not without danger. I never experienced anything more than clipping the top of a tree and a fuel pump failure, but others have made some pretty hard landings, mostly because of mechanical failure. One pilot told me that eventually every chopper pilot has crashed or is going to, so before you get on board always ask if he's got his crash out of the way. I did most of the elk counts in my district until the Division hired area biologists and then I flew as an observer and to keep the crew from getting lost.

Quality elk hunting

In the late 1970s and into the early 1980s hunters began changing their attitudes from purely utilitarian values of putting meat on the table toward the experience of hunting bull elk as they knew it back in the 1950s and earlier. The Wildlife Commission had established twenty quality elk hunting units across Colorado. In those units the Commission limited the number of bull elk hunting licenses. Within a few years the bull/cow ratio had improve dramatically. The opportunity to take a mature bull elk i n c r e a s e d and the hunting experience was enhanced by reducing the number of hunters.

The Wildlife Commission directed the Division to add another quality elk unit. Several units were considered. The quality of elk hunting was declining as over 4,000 elk hunters were crowding into the Upper Rio Grande game management unit 76. The area was 95% national forest land and one of the least populated areas in Colorado, but hunters were complaining about the hunting experience and the success ratio was declining.

I was concerned when I made the winter elk sex ratio count. I was classifying nearly 2,000 elk and there were very few bulls left. I was concerned that the calf production was declining, because there may not have been enough bulls to carry over into the next breeding season. I now think I was wrong. There were very few mature bulls, but enough yearling bulls were surviving to breed. The "quality" of the hunting experience had deteriorated by overcrowding hunters. Hunting is not a competitive activity.

Before implementing a plan that would reduce the number of hunters and impact the economy, the Division sought public involvement. Check station biologists interviewed resident and nonresident hunters to determine whether they would support a restriction that would possibly preclude their chances of drawing a license every year. There was overwhelming support by t h o s e leaving the area after a hunting season.

The most impacted people however were those who lived and worked in the Upper Rio Grande. I set up a public meeting. Before the meeting was even announced a petition had already circulated in Creede protesting the change to a quality hunting unit.

Some local people who had hunted the area for generations feared they would no longer be able to hunt in their own back yard.

I was caught in the middle between the Wildlife Commission's direction to have more quality elk hunting units, the Creede people and biology. I knew how important hunting was to local hunters. They were my friends and neighbors. I also knew there would be a negative economic impact on businesses, ranchers, and outfitters when the number of hunters coming to the area would be drastically reduced. I didn't campaign to sell a change, but tried to facilitate the discussion.

A hundred people gathered in the Creede gymnasium. I got a call on the radio that staff was going to be late. The crowd was already getting impatient when I took the microphone and started a conversation. One of the young men in the audience spoke out and asked "What will my young son say when he gets old enough to hunt and things stay as they are?" I answered with a question, "What do you think he'll say?" And the reply came, "Dad, this is stupid."

Some hunters said their families would starve to death if they couldn't kill an elk every year. So with this debate going strong, I asked that we tone it down and open our minds. I assured them that the Division had not made up its mind and that we wanted to dispel some rumors and have staff listen to their concerns.

There was a healthy debate following the staff's presentation. Changing the status quo had its upside. The hunting experience would be enhanced as well as the opportunity to take a mature bull elk. The biological cost was would the change in the population dynamics of the herd. To stay within the carrying capacity of the range the cow numbers would have to be decreased to accommodate more bulls. That translated into fewer calves being born and reduced the number of animals that could be harvested annually.

A preference point system that was used to limit cow licenses would also apply to bull licenses. This meant that hunters might only be able to hunt periodically. After twenty years it took six years for residents and twelve years for nonresidents to draw a license. For those who hunted cow elk, the change made little difference in getting a license. The economic impact to local merchants, ranchers and outfitters was significant. They had the most to lose, but overall supported the change. The audience still had mixed feelings, but there was enough support that the Division

staff made the recommendation to include the Upper Rio
G r a n d e as a premier quality elk hunting unit. Most hunters have
been pleased with the results

Bighorn sheep

Bighorn sheep had always lived in the Upper Rio Grande, but
early prospectors and disease had eliminated all but a small remnant
of fourteen bighorns on Pole Mountain. In 1977 I proposed
transplanting bighorns back to the area. The Forest Service said only
if I could prove that they had lived where I thought we would
release them. I interviewed about two dozen old timers who told me
about bighorns and other wildlife as far back
as 1900.

After
Six years
Of field
work
getting
four sites
on the
priority
list, the
Division
under the
leadership
of Jim
Olterman,
Regional
Biologist,
transplanted

*Thirty years later, descendants of the
1983 bighorn transplant in Seepage
Creek take a break*   Photo by Lois Jump

the first bighorns in 1983 on Seepage Creek. Over the next few years
three more transplants were made. When we made these
transplants I always invited the town's people to witness the
release. Charles Downing, the Creede High School science teacher,
brought his science class for those "teachable moments".

Thirty years later I had the pleasure and satisfaction of seeing the
healthy descendants of our efforts that reestablished the bighorns to
the Upper Rio Grande. More than 200 bighorns now call the Upper
Rio Grande home.

Wilderness

"A wilderness, in contrast with those areas where man and his own works dominate the landscape, is hereby recognized as an area where the earth and its community of life are untrammeled by man, where man himself is a visitor who does not remain."   The 1964 Wilderness Act

The Wilderness Act of 1964 established over 750 wilderness areas across America. Colorado is home to forty-three wilderness areas. Congress consolidated the San Juan Wilderness and t h e Upper Rio Grande Primitive Area into the Weminuche Wilderness Area. Establishing wilderness boundaries was a long and contentious process. Compromise and consensus building gave way to power plays by interest groups who had a stake in the outcome. Many organizations and agencies made recommendations to Congress, which authorizes wilderness areas on public land.

Having seen how devastating some logging practices and road construction had been to elk, I felt strongly that establishing a large wilderness area was needed in order to protect elk. Like other wildlife officers, I was concerned about the destruction of some of the most pristine wilderness left in Colorado. A fifty-year Forest Service road map of the Upper Rio Grande proposed construction of timber roads along ridges and riparian areas with spur roads in between them. Since logging roads were built with taxpayer money, the Forest Service said they had to be open to public vehicular access. Elk were being pushed out of historic calving and summer ranges. The timber industry recommended the wilderness boundary include those lands primarily above timberline, while wilderness advocates recommended even more land in wilderness.

At that time there were only two alternatives: wilderness designation or unrestricted access. There was no room for compromise or consensus for other alternatives.

I rode with other wildlife officers and biologists from the San Juan Basin and the Rio Grande taking legislators, wildlife commissioners, newspaper reporters and others on horseback trips so they could see firsthand the proposed Weminuche Wilderness. We wanted them to envision what road construction and logging would do to the landscape and wildlife. Working with Division biologists we drafted the Division's recommendation for wilderness designation based strictly on the impacts upon elk.

A congressional committee convened one of several hearings in the Creede High School gymnasium. Representatives from a wide spectrum of interests testified either in favor or against wilderness designation. Don Smith, a Division biologist, presented the State's position that favored wilderness designation and the boundaries that district officers had recommended. Congress established the Weminuche Wilderness in 1975 and enlarged t present size of 488,341 acres 1993. The wilderness boundary didn't satisfy the

District Officer Herb Browning, Assistant Director Laurence Riordan and Director Harry Woodward survey the Weminuche Wilderness circa 1968

Field trip viewing the Weminuche Wilderness from South River Peak

extreme views, but Congress did (in my opinion) find some middle ground.

The 130,000 acre La Garita Wilderness area north of Creede was established by Congress in 1964. This wilderness area is primarily in the Gunnison National Forest. When a proposal came forward to enlarge the LaGarita Wilderness to include lands on the

Rio Grande National Forest, the Forest Service followed the same process of gathering public input as well as the Division's recommendations. In 1993 the LaGarita wilderness was enlarged to include Wason and Silver Parks on the Rio Grande National Forest while allowing a long established four-wheel drive corridor to the unique Wheeler Geological Area to remain open to vehicles.

Congress established the 1969 National Environmental Policy Act (NEPA) which directed federal agencies to include other environmental considerations in their management plans. The Forest Service continued to accomplish its mission of managing the nation's forest lands, but with more consideration for ecological impacts. As wildlife officers, we had new opportunity to comment and recommend alternatives to their management plans from a wildlife perspective. Although I didn't always agree, it was a change going from an adversary to forest plans to that of a participant, working with the Forest Service on behalf of wildlife. I recommended that the Forest Service close some roads to protect elk calving areas and other areas for escape cover. We began a new era of cooperation.

I went on Forest Service sponsored field trips to learn how they were going to log certain areas. When the market for aspen developed, I suggested a team visit my old district in Mancos where the Forest Service had been managing aspen for several decades. We learned from their experience how to better manage aspen forests and avoid past mistakes.

Watershed specialists, landscape architects, biologists, and other Forest Service staff along with loggers and sawmill operators, became involved in planning timber sales and together we designed timber sales that were economical for logging, enhanced wildlife habitat, and watersheds, and reduced the visual impacts. From a wildlife standpoint, closing and re vegetating logging roads following the timber harvest was the most significant factor of a logging plan.

Much of the timber management plan became irrelevant when a spruce bark beetle epidemic killed most of the spruce forests in the Rio Grande and

San Juan National Forests and more of the plan went up in smoke with the West Fork Complex fire in 2013.

Wilderness designation has always been and always will be a controversial land use. The advent of all-terrain vehicles (ATVs) demanded more areas for this style of recreation. Vehicles have their place, but not necessarily every place. *Multiple Use* does not mean every use is appropriate on each acre of land. I believe that in many cases the Forest Service has found a balance between the extremes of having all the land open to vehicular access and those who would not allow any such travel. I think Aldo Leopold had it right when he wrote:

"We abuse land because we regard it as a commodity belonging to us. When we see land as a community to which we belong, we may begin to use it with love and respect."
Aldo Leopold, Sand County Almanac

You are now a hatchery superintendent

The Rifle Falls Fish Hatchery near Rifle, Colorado was closed in March of 1969 because of a water pollution lawsuit filed by downstream water users on Rifle Creek. I got a phone call to prepare the Creede hatchery to receive four million rainbow fingerlings and I would be the hatchery superintendent. Walt Hawkins, a fish culturist at the LaJara Fish Hatchery, helped me. Several fish trucks arrived in one day and unloaded the baby fish. I began the daily routine of feeding fish, cleaning screens, removing dead fish and scrubbing raceways. I didn't have much time in a day to attend to my normal duties.

The Division transferred Fish Culturist Mel Rose and his family to Creede in May, to supervise the operation until the fish were large enough to stock later that summer. I was really happy to have Mel run the operation so I could get on with my district responsibilities. Mel stocked some fish in nearby reservoirs, but most went to other fisheries and hatcheries around the state before closing the unit in July. I enjoyed raising fish, but it kept me tied down and I preferred doing my regular duties.

Squeezing life out of a cutthroat

The cutthroat trout is the only truly native trout in Colorado. A red slash below its jaw is the trait this beautiful fish is named for. Scientists have identified several subspecies of cutthroat in Colorado such as the Greenback native to the Arkansas, Colorado River cutthroat, and Rio Grande. Over the years other subspecies have been stocked from other river basins such as the Yellowstone and Snake Rivers.

For several years Mr. Humphreys, who owned Haypress Lake, had allowed the Division to take cutthroat spawn. He had a legacy of promoting the stocking of cutthroat trout. In 1968 I negotiated with him for a long term agreement to trade the taking of cutthroat eggs for some rainbows the Division would stock his private lake on Goose Creek. Mr. Humprey's daughter Ruth and husband Darcy Brown continued that agreement. Haypress Lake is now a Rio Grande cutthroat brood lake. At that time no attention was given to the hybridization of the cutthroat which had become genetic mix we called the native cutthroat.

Spawning a cutthroat

Every spring the cutthroats migrated up Grouse Creek to spawn. Area personnel dug small fish traps to catch spawning trout. When the fish were "ripe" area officers, fish biologists, and fish culturists came for the cutthroat squeezing party. We g e n t l y squeezed the females to release their eggs into small dish pans and then fertilized them with sperm from the males. The fish were released back into the lake. We normally took close to a million eggs that were taken to a fish hatchery.

One year the powers that be decided to hatch the Haypress Lake cutthroat eggs at the Creede hatchery. I became a hatchery superintendent once again. We got the water pump running and set up fish egg hatching incubators. I had hatchery responsibility all summer long. The state didn't hire any additional help, but Walt Hawkins helped several times a week. I still made time to check fishermen and patrol the district. We weren't on a forty-hour week then.

When fish eggs die they turn white and if not removed a fungus will infect the other eggs. Walt and I manually removed the dead eggs. The eggs Began to Hatch in July. After they absorbed their egg sacs, I fed

Stocking cutthroat in Weminuche Creek

fish several times a day and cleaned raceways every day and checked fishermen in between.

By September the cutthroats were almost two inches long and ready to be stocked. I prepared fish for back-country stocking by putting about a thousand fingerlings in a heavy duty plastic bag with a couple gallons of water. I inflated the bags with oxygen and sealed them with castrating rings and put them into empty fish food sacks, giving some insulation and protection. Dave Lemons arranged for me to stock fish by helicopter in the Upper Rio Grande high country waters that year.

Normally one of the fish hatcheries brought the cutthroat fingerlings to me and I delivered the fish to outfitters and other volunteers who were waiting at different trailheads. I packed remaining fish myself. Volunteers saved me a lot of days and miles to stock the high country creeks and beaver dams. I could never have done it by myself, but perhaps it was just as important for people to have a vested interest in their wildlife.

Regional pilots stocked most of the high country lakes. The Division had used this method since the 1940s. Thousands of man hours were saved every year compared to packing fish horseback. The technique is also very dangerous. On September 4, 2002 Jim Olterman, senior biologist and chief pilot, was stocking Hunt Lake west of Salida, Colorado when his Cessna was caught by a downdraft. Jim was killed in the crash. Brandon White, a Division employee, survived.

I enjoyed handling such beautiful fish, fertilizing eggs, witnessing the beginning of life and the developing eggs hatch; feeding the little ones, and releasing them into the wild. In a couple years only a few fish would survive. Anglers had no idea of the effort that went into raising the fish that they caught. I had a special satisfaction similar to what a farmer feels seeing a crop being harvested because of his efforts.

September was a great time to ride the high country whether stocking fish or checking archery hunters and fishermen. The pace slowed ever so slightly in September before the October big game seasons. Aspen leaves paved the trails with shades of yellow and gold. The fragrance of fallen leaves and the clean mountain air was exhilarating, but a harbinger of winter. After the first killing freeze, Indian Summer arrived with clear crisp mornings and mild afternoons. The sky turned to a cold azure blue. I always packed my jacket and saddle slicker just in case winter suddenly came over the mountain peaks.

The underwater world

My dad and I fished some lakes that were good one year and then the fish winterkilled. I became interested in fish winterkill research when our conservation club worked with biologist Don Nolting at Echo Lake south of Idaho Springs. When I got to the Creede district, Regional Fish Biologist Lloyd Hazzard was beginning a winterkill prevention project. We installed aerators and I helped Lloyd maintain them and assisted him with measuring oxygen levels and the effects of aerators. Hazzard demonstrated that there was real potential at Road Canyon Reservoir worthy of further study

Measuring dissolved oxygen levels

Bill Babcock, a Division Fisheries Researcher continued Hazzard's project by experimenting with different aeration systems. Babcock extended his study beyond Road Canyon to Regan Lake, which didn't have an electric line near the lake. Bill installed two windmill powered air compressors. In addition we tried gasoline powered engines and air compressors. Volunteers camped out in an old homesteader's cabin to attend to the compressors.

All this underwater equipment needed periodic maintenance. I had wanted to be a scuba diver since the 1950s television show "Sea Hunt". I decided to take care of the underwater maintenance myself. Although Beth didn't particularly enjoy water sports, we took a scuba diving course at the Glenwood Springs swimming pool. After we earned our certification we bought all the necessary equipment. We spent the money to do the job just like we paid for our own horses and tack.

When word got around that we were divers, we helped other officers and biologists with everything from underwater photography, to repairing a boat dock, and catching crawdads to transplant into Road Canyon Reservoir. We explored the underwater world in several high mountain lakes to get a fish eye perspective of their habitat, but mostly we maintained underwater aerators.

I did some diving to assist local water users with their dams. The Division had a conservation pool agreement with the LaGarita Ranch for Trout Lake which was in the Weminuche Wilderness Area. The water rights and dam preceded wilderness designation, but required periodic inspection and maintenance. Water was leaking through the outlet valve.

I helped ranchers like Dan Anderson of the La Garita Ranch repair underwater valves on dams. Dan packed our scuba gear twelve miles to Trout Lake. I dove to the bottom of the lake and removed a rock that had jammed the valve. Dan was able to close the valve and we saved the conservation pool in this wilderness reservoir. We provided a cutthroat fishery and enhanced the beauty of the whole basin. The Division traded some of its water to the ranch for the conservation pool. It was a win-win agreement for the Division, the ranch, the fish, fishermen, and the wilderness.

Word of my scuba diving work got around to the sheriffs in the Valley. The Conejos County Sheriff asked me to search for a stolen safe that he thought had been dumped into a canal, but it was too dangerous and I suggested they search when the water was turned out of the canal.

The Costilla County Sheriff asked me to search for a drowning victim in Smith Reservoir. The limited visibility a n d aquatic weed growth was too great to safely search. About that time I got acquainted with a Rio Grande County Sheriff Deputy who was a diver and together we started the San Luis Valley Underwater Recovery Team. The Valley sheriffs went together and purchased dry diving suits for the two of us and we took a training course to learn how to safely use them. Other divers joined us and made several body and property recoveries.

Water for wildlife

Since the 1950s the Division had purchased and built several lakes and reservoirs in the Upper Rio Grande. These provided some excellent fishing and helped the local economy. Water is a precious commodity in Colorado and the Division invested sportsmen's money to develop some water resources for wildlife. The Division purchased three transmountain water diversions from ranchers that transported water from the San Juan and Gunnison basins into the Rio Grande. These were small volume diversions that did n o t dewater the streams below them.

Southwest Regional Fish Biologist Lloyd Hazzard and Mike Zgainer (the officer in South Fork at the time) were instrumental in negotiating conservation pool agreements with ranchers who owned water storage rights in eight reservoirs and seven that the Division owned. The Division traded some Division water to ranchers to irrigate their Crops in exchange for leaving enough water in their reservoirs to sustain fisheries. We also traded water to stabilize wetlands in the Valley floor.

It was a win-win arrangement. In case the Division couldn't deliver the

Changing the water recorder chart on Piedra Diversion circa 1970

agreed amount of water, then the water user was free to use his or her water right. The Division invested hundreds of thousands of dollars for the diversions.

I had the responsibility to maintain the diversions every week during the summer. I changed the water charts and took them to the state engineer's office. This meant a lot of time horseback, hiking shovel work, plugging up gopher holes and sand bagging washouts. I was relieved when the Division hired wildlife technicians who took over the maintenance of the diversions.

The Spring Creek Diversion was located on the Continental Divide at Spring Creek Pass where State Highway149 crosses the Continental Divide. The Piedra Diversion was at the edge of the Weminuche Wilderness and was accessible by horseback or hiking from the end of a jeep road.

Deep snowdrifts blocked the diversion of decreed water until the snow all melted. In the 1980s the Division proposed a major project to bury pipelines. The three ditches that diverted water were inside the boundary of the Weminuche Wilderness. Burying pipelines would require the use of mechanized equipment, which is prohibited inside a wilderness, but since the water right predated wilderness designation the Division went through a complicated process to get approval from the Forest Service. The Division got approval to use a backhoe to bury the pipelines. As a training exercise the Army used a Chinook helicopter to fly a backhoe to the diversion, which is 12,000 feet above sea level.

The Division's third diversion transported water from the headwater

Piedra cabin   circa June, 1970

Pine River across Weminuche Pass and down to the Rio Grande. It was a six mile horseback trip to maintain the ditch and change the recorder chart. All work on this diversion was done by hand. No mechanized equipment could be used   for maintenance. Electronic technology now transmits water volume data using solar powered transmission via satellite to the State Engineer's office, which saves a lot of days in the saddle retrieving that important data.

The general public has little idea of the financial investment the Division has made to protect water resources for wildlife. It is so easy to take for granted the work that we did to provide lakes and reservoirs for recreation such as fishing. All the while the Division was developing these resources; we were also the best neighbor that ranchers and farmers, who were also water users, ever had. We were partners working together. This didn't mean that everyone w a s happy with all that the Division did with other issues, but when it came to water we worked together as much as possible.

Making the most of a temporary situations

Some of the old-timers in Creede told me that the Seepage Lakes had been a commercial fishery at one time. These two lakes were appropriately named. During a wet cycle of precipitation the Santa Maria Reservoir water level rose high enough for water to seep through a geological fault and surface in Seepage Creek. Following the winter of 1978-79, an above average snowfall and runoff filled these two small reservoirs. I sneaked some catchable-sized rainbows (10 inch fish) from a couple fish trucks and stocked some fingerlings into the lakes. I didn't tell anyone, but someone must have seen some fish rising the next year and the fishing frenzy was on   The lakes had a tremendous forage base of salamanders and all the worms, grubs, and other organisms common to a flooded cattle grazing allotment. The fish grew at an amazing rate for three years. The largest fish almost broke the state record for a rainbow trout of eighteen pounds. For a couple years fishermen were catching many lunkers.

The sub terrain leaked water like a sieve and when the wet cycle ended, the lakes dried up and the great fishing was but a memory. Nowadays such an experiment would be frowned on because of whirling disease. The economic and biological risk I took was minimal. The benefit was temporary, but we made a lot of people happy and when you can make a fisherman smile that's quite an accomplishment.

In the 1973 the state leased the Hartman Fish Hatchery [originally the Hosselkus Fish Hatchery and currently the Mountain

View Resort and RV Park] to operate as a brood fish station. Bob Little, a Division fish culturist ran the operation. He took fish eggs from brood fish, hatched them, and the fingerlings were transferred to other state fish hatcheries to grow to catchable size of about ten inches. When old brood fish don't produce eggs Bob culled them and we sneaked some of them into nearby Spring Creek Pond and Love Lake. Most of the culled brood fish were transferred to the Durango Fish Hatchery and stocked along with their catchable sized fish to "spice up" the fishing experience for anglers in the San Juan Basin.

I got up early the morning after we stocked those five to eight pound brood fish in Spring Creek Pond and hid in the trees to watch. The first fishermen were a grandpa and his grandson. The boy cast his line out and he immediately hooked one of those lunkers. When the lad landed the fish, grandpa grabbed the fish, the boy, and threw them into the car and sped off. Within an hour the lake was surrounded by fishermen and by noon I bet most of those lunkers had been caught. The Division closed the brood fish operation in 1978 and Bob went on to be the superintendent of the Durango Fish Hatchery. Grandpas, grandkids and big fish make good memories.

Guides and Outfitters

In the late 1960s the General Assembly (GA) decided that outfitters needed to be regulated. Because most outfitters guided hunters and fishermen, the GA dumped another responsibility or the Division and down to the district officers. Professional outfitters were concerned about outlaw operators who were ripping off clients with false promises, outright fraud and giving the business a bad reputation.

I didn't know anything about the outfitting business, other than I worked with some of the best. I felt kind of awkward giving tests to professional outfitters who were teaching me about their business. All outfitters and their guides had to take a first aid course before they got a license. Outfitters who provided services on federal lands had to get permits from the Forest Service or BLM. They had to post a bond, be insured, and pay fees to the government for every client they took onto federal lands. Those who leased private ranches paid the landowner for a lease. The overhead put some outfitters out of business. The legislature put the Division of Professions and Occupations in charge of licensing outfitters in 2012.

I had witnessed a number of novice hunters, fishermen and other outdoors people who were poorly equipped and ill prepared to be in the wilderness. At best they were miserable and at the worst they were in dangerous circumstances. I rode up Squaw Creek the day before elk season. It had snowed about four inches and was slowing lightly. I rode into a camp of four hunters who had backpacked about four miles. They were huddled in a four man nylon tent and for heat they had a two burner Coleman stove and two gallons of fuel. I asked them how they were going to stay warm when they ran out of gas. I told them that a storm was coming in and I suggested they break camp and go to lower country and find a resort with an available cabin.

Contrast that camp with the next one up the trail which had a large cook tent with a space heater and a large stack of firewood and a tent for sleeping. Later in the day when I came back down the trail there were ten inches of snow and I was relieved that they had taken my advice and broke camp and left.

Time and again I saw the benefits that professional outfitters provided to their clients: a dry camp, a full belly, and in some cases a sore butt. The outfitters I worked with in the Upper Rio Grande provided outstanding service to the public. I never had a serious complaint from clients or from the Forest Service. I was always welcome in their camps and found most of them intolerant of even their own clients violating the hunting and fishing laws. Outfitters enjoyed sharing the wilderness with their clients by providing them with life changing experiences.

Checking some rainbow trout at Ruby Lake with a guest and outfitter Charlie Kipp

An outfitter sometimes asked a client to surrender his or her watch, daily planner and nowadays the smart phone for a few days to live without all vestiges of civilization. I advise the novice against going alone into the wilderness, because it can kill   you. Rather, venture forth with someone who knows how to not only survive, but also how to maximize the wilderness experience. Going with a pro can be the ultimate experience for a novice as well as a seasoned mountaineer.

One day I stopped at a trailhead where Charlie Kipp was in the final stages of getting his pack train ready to hit the trail. His dudes were saddled up and ready to go. "Doc" Barksdale M.D. was riding along to help Charlie. In addition to being experienced help along the trail and in camp, "Doc" was in charge of entertainment and morale. His sense of humor and wit made for good PR to convince a client, "You're going to enjoy this whether you like it or not."

"Doc" was on his horse with his medical bag hanging from the saddle horn. I teasingly asked him if he had a first aid card. He answered, "Yes, and this time I remembered to bring extra death certificates." Charlie chimed, "I packed an extra shovel. The look on those dudes' faces changed like when a black cloud suddenly blocks the sun. They didn't know whether to dismount right then or not. Charlie assured them that he would take good care of them. I knew they were in good hands and would have an enjoyable and memorable pack trip with Charlie and Doc. I had that confidence in all my outfitters.

Conservation camp

The Colorado State University Extension Service sponsored a youth conservation camp held each spring at a Boy Scout camp in South Fork. The U.S. Forest Service, Fish and Wildlife Service, Natural Resource Conservation Service, State Forest Service, The Division and dozens of volunteers took on the challenge of teaching sixty kids from the Valley. We taught forestry, range management, wildlife, and other aspects of natural resource conservation.

Dave Kenvin and I took our wildlife kids on field trips for hands on experiences. We had them electro fish a creek, identify and evaluate the habitat. They used telemetry equipment to search for radio collared bighorn sheep. We arranged for a fish truck and they stocked fish in the Rio Grande. Every year we took advantage of teachable moments.

The Monte Vista Wildlife Refuge personnel trapped some Canada geese for the kids to catch and band. The kids came alongside professional natural resource managers just as I had experienced in my high school conservation club. At the end of each camp the kids gave a show and tell presentation to their parents. The time we spent with kids was a good investment. Wildlife officers throughout Colorado participate in conservation camps and outdoor education programs.

The divergence of merging trails

Politicians don't always make sense either. The Colorado General Assembly (GA) changed the name of the Game and Fish Department to The Game, Fish and Parks Department in 1963. The name change meant little to me at the time. There weren't any state parks even close to my district. Soon after I was transferred to Creede however, I began to experience the additional work load of being a park ranger.

I found myself enforcing boat registration, regulations, and doing safety inspections. When the public started snowmobiling, I enforced snowmobile registration and regulations. The GA decided that since a few youngsters had been injured while driving snowmobiles that we needed to have snowmobile safety classes in each district and that "duty as assigned" fell into the laps of district officers.

Whenever there was an advertised snowmobile event, State Park Rangers were supposed to be there to check registrations. The San Luis Valley Snowmobile Club sponsored an annual rally from Creede to Lake City. Over a hundred snowmobilers participated, which was a big event in those days. Club volunteers checked participants at both ends of the route to ensure everyone was accounted for. I checked the snowmobile registrations.

As the public became more and more motorized the GA decided to license trail bikes. Again, the registration and law enforcement duties were dumped on wildlife officers. During those years that the Game, Fish and Parks Department existed I never saw a State Park Ranger in my district. Hunting and fishing license money was paying for state park functions.

In 1973 the federal government threatened to withhold payments of the Pittman-Robertson and Dingell-Johnson federal funds from Colorado. In order to receive those funds a state is required to spend hunting and fishing license money only on wildlife. Keeping expenditures separated in an agency with dual missions is at best problematic. The GA consolidated State Parks and Wildlife into a single agency once again in 2012. Some administrative functions can be shared, but most field operations have remained separated. Park Rangers manage recreation in state parks and wildlife officers attend to wildlife.

Giggles

I was checking fishermen up at Rio Grande Reservoir one day. The reservoir had been drawn down and it was a long steep hike to get back up the road. I saw a man hiking up toward to the road, so I let him come to me.

When he got up to the road, he was out of breath. He approached me and with the best impersonation of WC Fields [an actor during the 1930s and '40s] caught his breath and exclaimed, "Stand back sonny. . . I'm going to take one breath and suck all the air out of this canyon." When I checked his fishing license I noted he was from Los Angeles, which was noted for its smog. I asked him if he was enjoying our clean mountain air and he replied, "I don't trust air I can't see and my lungs are used to chewing."

Working with the public all the time, you learn to read people. I was checking a fisherman and he complained, "I have fished for three days and haven't caught anything. If there was a fish in this river, I could catch it." I told him that a fisherman who was just down the river was catching fish. Then, I told him that I was going to have to arrest him and in shock asked, "For what?" I told him he was under arrest for "impersonating a fisherman." He raised his hands, and placed them onto my pickup and said, "I'm guilty, you caught me fair and square." The tension broke and he laughed and asked me if I could write him a ticket as a souvenir. So I wrote him a phony ticket for "impersonating a fisherman" and he was as happy as could be. For being a good sport I gave him one of my favorite flies and some tips on how to start catching fish. I used this ploy many times to lighten up fishing and hunting contacts.

CHAPTER 10
Horses, hitches and rocky trails

The first summer I worked in the Upper Rio Grande was one of excitement and adventure (they all were). After being cooped up all winter it was time to explore my mountain paradise. Some of my favorite memories are from the many days and miles I rode the high country. Some days were pure pleasure and others were cold, wet, and miserable times in the saddle. Horses were a necessity for an officer who was assigned to a district that had wilderness or roadless back country. If an officer wanted horses he paid for them himself as well as tack gear, and veterinarian bills. The Division paid for grain, hay, pasture, horse shoeing and provided a horse trailer.

I could check some of the high lakes and streams in a day ride of twelve to twenty miles. I periodically walked to give my horse some relief as well as my knees and butt. When I rode patrols that took several days, I camped out.

When I checked fishermen's licenses and fish I also noted the condition of the fish, because they grow slowly in high altitude lakes and over stocking a lake can lead to stunted growth rates.

Cooking supper over a campfire

When I rode to a particular lake or creek I didn't know for sure if any fishermen would even be there. So, I carried a pack rod and some flies in case I needed to personally sample the fish population to ensure the waters were properly stocked. Being as dedicated as I was I went a step further than necessary by keeping a fish or two for supper to make sure they were safe to eat. I had more than one angler ask, "Do you get paid to do this?" (And, yes I always had a fishing license.)

Working with horses has some inherent danger. Horse related injuries were one of the leading causes of Workman's Compensation claims with the Division

Beth said, "I really only worried about you when you were riding horses." S o m e t i m e s she rode with me when I changed water charts on the diversions, stocked fish, or checked fishermen. She didn't ride with me during hunting seasons.

Our family was as normal as any in Creede. When the kids were teenagers they got jobs. Ralph wrangled horses and did odd jobs while Lois worked at local restaurants. Lois played volleyball and Ralph wrestled. Even before they were teenagers I took the family with me on a working packtrip each summer. I

Family taking a lunch break in an alpine flower garden at Donut Lake. Mt Silex and Storm King Mt. across the canyon <u>*Weminuche Wilderness circa 1975*</u>

checked fishermen and contacted people as usual. Our f a m i l y enjoyed these trips together and we made good memories (like the time I forgot the cook kit.)

The day I lost my lunch

I was riding up the Squaw Creek trail to check fishermen at Squaw Lake. When I came to a long meadow next to the creek I decided to eat my lunch before climbing the switchbacks through the tall timber to the lake. Pet was just moseying up the trail when I pulled my lunch out of the saddle bag and spread it out in my lap. I looped the reins around the saddle horn and was enjoying an easy lunch on the trail. It doesn't get any better than this.

I got thirsty and reached into my saddle bag for a Pepsi. The soda pop was warm and had been shaken, so when I popped the top, cola shot out of the can. Then things commenced to happening really fast. Pet took off like a bear was at her heals. The reins went flying as did my lunch. As I slid back over the cantle I grabbed the saddle horn and somehow managed to pull myself back into the saddle. I grabbed the flying reins and slowly pulled on the brakes. Idiosyncrasy number one: Pet didn't like Pepsi. The ravens enjoyed my lunch. I think I heard God chuckle.

Real cowboys wear spurs

I felt that I had an image to maintain, so I wore a Stetson, chaps, western boots and spurs. Gene Riggs and I packed some cutthroats up to the headwaters of Ivy Creek. After stocking the fingerlings in the meandering little creek, we headed back down the canyon. There was no trail so Gene led the way, with pack horse in tow, bushwhacking our way through downed timber. As Pet rounded an uprooted spruce tree, she jammed my boot and spur into her flank. The next thing I did was a loop-to-loop and landed flat on my back. I saw stars.

Gene called down to me, "Are ya hurt?" I moved my toes, so I thought I was okay. Pet just stood there grazing, having rid herself of a pain in her side. I climbed back into the saddle and pain racked my body. It hurt to ride and it hurt to walk the six miles to the trailhead. Idiosyncrasy number two: Pet didn't like spurs.

Later the doctor said that my being bruised, sore, and stiff were typical of rodeo injuries. I still wince when I watch bucking bulls and broncs throw their riders. I didn't wear spurs anymore. I wasn't a cowboy. They just gave me the hat. I soon bought Diamond, a brown quarter horse with a white diamond on his forehead. Pet and Diamond worked together and I could ride or pack either one of them. In all the years and thousands of miles that I rode, I was never seriously hurt.

Don't ever tell the warden "We're over the limit."

One of my favorite horse patrols was around the Ute Creek basin. There are six Ute Lakes and about twenty miles of good creek and beaver dam fishing. In addition I checked Donut, Hidden, Flint, and Rock Lakes just over the Divide. I worked out of a good campsite along the trail below the Twin Ute Lakes.

One evening I had eaten supper, picketed Pet for the n i g h t, and was sitting by my campfire. As dusk turned to black dark I saw the glow of a cigarette coming down the trail. Three young men walked into my camp. In the darkness they didn't recognize who I was.

These lads were real friendly and offered me some fish, ". . . because we're over the limit." I offered to count their fish. I identified myself and told them they were indeed over the limit. One of them was carrying a pistol and I took it away from him and unloaded it. I wrote one of them a mail-in Penalty Assessment (PA). [The legislature established the Penalty Assessment by assessing a fine for more common violations. An officer had the discretion to issue a mail-in PA, write a summons or take a defendant to jail.]

I returned the pistol and they hiked on down the trail to their camp. When you're fifteen miles from the nearest trailhead it would be cruel and unusual punishment to make the defendant hike that far and drive thirty miles to mail in his fine for what was usually a minor violation. If the fine wasn't paid, the county judge issued a bench warrant for an arrest. I never had one go unpaid.

"Sic em!"

When I rode the high country checking fishermen, I contacted more people who were just enjoying backpacking, camping, photographing the scenery, and having a good time in the wilderness. I enjoyed helping folks have a good time. I answered questions and once in a while administered first aid.

One day I was riding through a spectacular wilderness garden of Colorado columbine flowers. A small group of backpackers was walking toward me. I dismounted and greeted them. One of the party asked, "How often to the gardeners come up to care for these gardens?" I told her that they were God's gardens that He cares for. She said, "No, I'm serious." To which I replied, "So am I." For someone used to manicured gardens in the big city, I can understand being overwhelmed with the beauty of the natural world.

I never had a fisherman or hunter threaten or assault me in the high country until the day I was riding down to the forks of Ute Creek trail and came upon a lone backpacker who was hiking with his dog. I greeted him with a "howdy" and he returned my salutation by commanding his dog, "Sic em!"

His big black dog bared his teeth and lunged toward Pet and me. Pet started dancing around and I pulled my jacket back and put my hand on my .357 and I told him to call his dog off or I'd kill him [the dog]. He pled, "Please don't kill my dog." He immediately called his dog off. The dog obeyed and heeled.

I gathered my wits, got Pet settled down, and dismounted. Knowing I was armed, he was justifiably scared. Then I identified myself. He didn't know what I was going to do with him. I told him that I could arrest him for assault, handcuff him, march him ten miles to the trailhead and take him to jail. He was shaking.

I settled instead for a royal chewing out (not a cussing out). He hadn't thought of the consequences of hurting another person. He apologized and I turned him loose. With his head hung down he hiked on up the trail.

As I got back in the saddle and rode off it occurred to me that if I'd fired my pistol while on Pet, there was no way that I would have hit the dog and she probably would have thrown me to the top of the closest tree which was a quarter of a mile away and if I survived that, I'd had to hike ten miles to my truck.

It was just a little scratch

In 1969 I took a pack trip from Wolf Creek Pass to Trout Lake with several other wildlife officers to show Division staff, some legislators, wildlife commissioners and a couple journalists the heart of the proposed Weminuche Wilderness Area. At the beginning of the trip I scratched my finger when I checked Pet's shoes. It was just a little scratch and I ignored it, but each day my finger became more swollen and painful.

On our last morning I felt feverish. By the time I got home I had a 102 degree fever. Red streaks ran up my arm. Beth drove me to the doctor in Del Norte. I had a bad case of blood poisoning. Dr. Mannring gave me a shot of penicillin in each hip and called the drug store after hours to get me more antibiotics.

I remember it was July 20, 1969, a historical day because that evening we watched on television as astronaut Neil Armstrong stepped onto the moon and said his famous line, "That's one small step for a man . . . one giant leap for mankind." It took a couple days for the swelling and fever to subside and I never ignored another scratch.

The moon landing took on more meaning a couple years later when I visited Ralph Conkey's elk hunting camp. One of his hunters that I checked was Michael Collins, the Lunar Command Module pilot who orbited the moon while Neil Armstrong and Buzz Aldrin explored the moon's surface. Collins gave me a commemorative medallion of that first moon mission.

The big chase

For decades Costilla County in the southeastern side of the Valley was a poaching hotbed. Before the Forbes Trinchera, Taylor, and Vermejo Park became ranches they were Spanish land grants. For generations, families had gathered firewood and killed elk and deer for sustenance. A small segment of the population called themselves "traditional hunters" who felt it still their right to kill animals whenever they wanted. Although private landowners don't own the wildlife on their property, they do have the right to control their land and deny access. Ranchers found their fences cut, gates torn down, and property vandalized.

In an attempt to stem the poaching in the summer we patrolled horseback along the divide between the Valley and the Purgatory River drainage southwest of La Veta, Colorado. The Division made arrangements with Vermejo Park for the use of a cabin near the New Mexico-Colorado state line for our base came. Lonnie Brown and I rode horse back every day looking for poachers. We knew that anyone we contacted would be armed so we wore sidearms and carried rifles in our saddle scabbards. This was serious and dangerous work.

On the last day of our patrol we hit the trail early to check for fresh horse tracks on a route that trespassers and poachers used. We rode down into some timber where we could see a large meadow and listen for rifle shots. We saw a few elk and took in the beautiful scene that lay below us. All was quiet. The elk drifted into the timber and we decided to ride back to the cabin, clean up, load our horses and head for home.

As we rode uphill to the timberline, I reined Diamond to a stop. Above and ahead of us were five armed horsemen. They hadn't spotted us and fortunately Diamond didn't whinny to say, "Hello." With adrenaline running high, Lonnie and I held back just in case they might just kill some elk right in front of us. But, it was late enough in the morning that the elk were already bedded down in the timber until evening. Sure enough the horsemen rode back into San Francisco Creek, but we knew they hadn't seen us and believed they would be back later in the day.

From high on the mountain we had radio contact with our packset. Lonnie called for backup officers. Those of us who worked along the state line also had federal game warden commissions so we could enforce wildlife laws in either state. We waited above timberline on top of the mountain where we could see anyone coming into the area. While we were waiting, a thunderstorm came through and lightning flashed around us. There was no place to hide and it soon passed. That in itself was an electrifying experience.

Rusty Forbes, the South East Regional Pilot, heard our radio transmission and flew down our way and asked for our location and he buzzed us, nearly starting a rodeo. He asked where we thought our suspects were and we told him. He pulled flaps on his Cessna and glided down San Francisco Creek and dipped his wings pointing to the poachers' camp.

We assumed that they knew they had been discovered. By then Vermejo Park Ranch manager, Pat McGraw, New Mexico Game and Fish Department supervisor Tim Barraclaugh, and two of his WCOs had joined us. We gave up the idea of waiting for the poachers to go hunting.

We had backup officers preparing an ambush lower down San Francisco Creek. We took off after them. We found their abandoned campfire still burning. Their trail was obscure at first, but before long we were on an abandoned logging road and as we were soon galloping and jumping over downed logs like it was a steeplechase. We didn't know where our backup had set up the ambush. We were at a full gallop when we came around a bend in the road and there they were standing in a little meadow.

We had not discussed what we would do if we caught them, because we thought we'd just

A New Mexico WCO stands guard as we interrogate poachers

follow them into the ambush.

You can imagine what these hombres must have thought as six armed men came up on them so fast. I reined Diamond back and as we bounced to a stop I yelled at them to put their hands up. We didn't think they had any game with them, but they were trespassing. Nevertheless, we disarmed them and ordered them to sit while we searched their packs.

I asked the man who appeared to be the leader, what they were doing back there. Dumb question, but I thought I'd ask. He answered, "We were just taking a day ride to show the boys the country." I replied, "It takes pack horses, rifles, tents, food, sleeping bags, meat sacks, skinning and boning knives to take a day ride?" He answered, "Hey man, you never know when it might rain." We escorted them down the trail and into the ambush where we were immediately surrounded by armed wildlife officers. They knew we meant business, but all we could cite them for was trespassing. I'm sure they laughed at us when the county judged fined them ten dollars. But, they knew we could be out there any time, any place.

I rode on two other patrols with officers Dave Hoart and Bob Holder, but we never saw another person. Other officers patrolled and only a few contacts were ever made. We worked day and night year after year to stem the crimes against wildlife. For all our efforts we had little success against the poachers, but we never gave up. Read on: A time for wildlife justice was coming.

Paddling down the trail

The Rio Grande as well as other major rivers in Colorado had been world class fisheries. As the years passed the quality of fishing had deteriorated. Hatchery raised rainbows returned to the creel, but most did not survive the wild rigors of a river. The days of wild jumping, thrashing rainbows were becoming echoes of the past. If hatchery fish were any dumber they wouldn't have known how to swim.

The Wildlife Commission implemented more quality fishing regulations to improve the number and size of wild fish that successfully spawned in good habitats. Increasing regulations required more law enforcement. Patrolling more waters, especially those not easily accessible added to our workload. I saw a television program featuring Idaho WCOs patrolling the Middle Fork of the Salmon River in kayaks. That spawned the idea of doing the same on the Rio Grande. Dave Kenvin and I decided to start the Rio Grande

Navy. Other officers started patrolling other rivers about the same time.

Bruce "Buck" Stroh, a high school business teacher in Creede, was an experienced kayaker. He agreed to teach Dave and me how to kayak. The Division didn't have a budget to purchase such equipment so the San Luis Valley Chapter of Trout Unlimited raised the money and purchased our kayaks, spray skirts, paddles, air bags, wet suits, life jackets and helmets. We trained in the Monte Vista community swimming pool.

Checking fishermen in kayaks was pure pleasure, punctuated by moments of pure unadulterated terror. Such was the case when one day Dave and I shoved off from Seven Mile Campground to patrol the Rio Grande. We had just paddled a short distance when we suddenly saw a fence stretched across the river. Ranchers sometimes stretched fences

A fisherman shows me his license

across rivers to contain grazing cattle on their land, but this fence was intended to keep rafters from floating across private land. It was a death trap. Dave was ahead of me and had to bail out of his kayak to avoid getting caught in the fence. He swam to shore. We later found his boat and paddle down river. It was a close call.

That same summer I was floating with four expert white water canoeists who wanted to paddle the Box Canyon of the Rio Grande below Rio Grande Reservoir. This six mile stretch of river flows through the Weminuche Wilderness. It was one of the most difficult stretches of river on which to check fishermen. The kayak gave us the ability to check fishermen that had never been checked.

When the river is fishable, it is a thrilling technical paddle to bob, weave, and careen through boulder fields, rapids, and plunge over little waterfalls. I checked fishermen and wrote one fishermen for not having a fishing license, while they cavorted in the white water.

As we maneuvered through the next set of rapids, my kayak was suddenly pinned sideways against a boulder like it was a rock magnet. I was in serious trouble. This can be fatal if the kayak collapses and pins your legs so you can't escape. Fortunately, my kayak didn't collapse, so I braced my paddle upstream to hold myself out of the water, hyperventilated, held my breath, pulled the spray skirt and rolled underwater and out of the kayak. I popped up and was swept into the eddy below the boulder. I gasped for air as my kayak came loose on its own and I caught it in the eddy. I held onto my paddle, got back into the boat and continued on. My paddle buddies saw my dilemma and were ready to rescue me.

It was quite a surprise for many fishermen when Dave and I paddled over to them and announced, "We're District Wildlife Managers for the Colorado Division of Wildlife. We'd like to check your fishing license and fish please." Responses were most interesting. There were anglers like one old timer who said, "I've been fishing for fifty years on this river and never had my license checked." He produced a license and was pleased we were checking. That summer I checked him so many times that by summer's end we were on a first name basis. He said that told everyone he knew to buy a license and we never caught another angler without a license in that section where he fished.

While kayaking the Conejos River one angler confessed, "I have a New Mexico fishing license." To which Dave called out in a loud voice, "Stand back everybody. We're going to see how far this man can cast!" As I wrote him a citation I asked him if he had any previous violations in Colorado. He answered that he had been caught fishing without a license a few years before on the Upper Rio Grande. When I took my helmet off he said, "You again?" Another slow learner bit the dust

I did overhear one complaint that, "It isn't fair that these game wardens are getting so sneaky." Dave and I kayaked other rivers in the region with other officers who were using kayaks to check fishermen. It was an effective method of contacting people and made the job even more fun. Within a couple years we noticed a decline in the number of fishing violations on those rivers.

Most of the La Garita Wilderness Area was in the Lake City and Saguache districts, so I didn't venture into the area very often. I wanted to learn some of that country better, so during a bighorn sheep season Beth and I saddled Pet and Diamond and rode up West Willow Creek above timberline, over the Divide, across the headwaters of Cascade Creek and into the headwaters of Saguache Creek into the heart of the wilderness. This is good bighorn country. Finally we found a camp of two bighorn hunters in Diabalo Canyon. We set up camp and soon the hunters came back to camp. They hadn't seen any sheep nor had we. We shared some campfire time and turned in for the night.

Early the next morning Beth and I rode over to Machin Lake and as we rode we heard several blasts of dynamite off in the distance. We rode on and soon we came upon a Forest Service trail crew building trail. No wonder there were no sheep in that area. There weren't any fishermen at Machin Lake either. I could see big cutthroats cruising the shallows searching for any morsel that fell into the crystal clear water. I was looking for sheep hunters and didn't take a fishing rod.

We rode back into the Rio Grande side of the Wilderness at Bonito Pass and camped for the night in Wason Park. It was fall and the night air was crisp.

We concluded our patrol across Wason Park and Down to Phoenix Park on The East Fork of Willow Creek. This had been one of those patrols

Glen looking for bighorn hunters in the Machin Lake Basin La Garita Wilderness

that one should feel guilty about getting paid for, but somebody has to do it.

My typical camp:
3 person nylon tent, single burner gas stove, freeze dried food, sleeping bag and pad, cook kit, an extra pair of socks, a ticket book, raincoat, jacket, and little else

CHAPTER 11
The two-edged sword

When you get hungry you go to the kitchen. If your kitchen has no food, you go to the grocery store. If you are immobile then someone has to bring food to you. Life is further threatened if the kitchen or the grocery store is destroyed. This is the dilemma that deer, elk, and other animals face in harsh winters. Some developments have destroyed the elk and deer "kitchen" and have fragmented their habitat, which compromises their survival during harsh winters. Add to that human activities such as ATV and snowmobile riders dressed in Darth Vader costumes roaring across the landscape, further disrupting their home territory.

By 1900 unregulated hunting of elk had wiped out some local elk populations. The Colorado General Assembly closed the elk hunting season in 1903 and reopened it in most areas by the late 1930s. Nationwide, sportsmen began to organize and demand wildlife conservation.

Congress established The National Elk Refuge in Jackson Hole, Wyoming in 1912. Outfitters, businesses, and the public demanded that the elk population be maintained above the land's biological carrying capacity. The government began feeding elk in the winter. Politics trumped biological wisdom. The public came to accept the feeding of elk and the National Elk Refuge had become a tourist attraction. Most biologists hold firm to the principle that feeding elk, deer and Other wildlife increases disease transmission and their dependence on humans all the while robbing them of their very wildness.

My first experience with feeding elk came in the winter of 1968-69. Early winter

Mixing elk pellets with hay

snowfall had blanketed the Upper Rio Grande. Most of the elk were getting along fine except for one herd in Miners Creek. I reported that about eighty head of elk were showing signs of malnutrition. Don Benson, my supervisor and "Smoky" Till our Regional Manager and I, met with the Creede Rotary Club before the people were aware that a problem was developing. Because of the experience in 1964, the Department's research section in conjunction with the Colorado State University Cooperative Wildlife Research Center had developed a nutritious and digestible pellet for elk. The ration however, had never been tested on wild elk.

We explained that we were going to experiment with the new pellet. I didn't know what I was doing, but supervised the operation. Charlie Kipp taught me how to get the elk to eat the pellets by mixing the pellets with some hay. The Division provided me with a Kristi Snowcat and a sled. Volunteers rode in the sled scattering hay and pellets. The elk took to the strange pellets within a couple d a y s . I began finding a few dead elk after just a few weeks. I necropsied several carcasses. The animals had fat and their stomachs were full. The tissue samples I sent to the Research Center revealed that the ration was probably too rich. Although more elk survived because we fed them, others died because we fed them. The pellet was modified and has been used successfully in other feeding operations since then.

When we moved to Creede someone told me that there were really only two seasons: Winter and the 4th ^{of} July. The winter of 1978-79 was the worst I ever experienced. The snow was deeper than the fence

posts from November to April. It was a bitter cold winter. The temperature dropped to 54 degrees below zero. School was

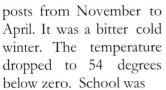

Creede School closed because of 54 below zero temperature circa 1979

closed because they couldn't keep the classrooms warm enough for the students.. Cars wouldn't start unless an engine heater was plugged in.

Fishermen are a hardy breed, not too smart sometimes, but hardy. They drove snowmobiles to the lower elevation lakes and reservoirs where they drilled holes through up to four feet of ice.

The state issued me a snowmobile so I could keep a watchful eye on them. They'd be out there enjoying a day

County Road Supervisor Paul Hosselkus plows the road up to our house on a cold wintry morning   circa 1979

of ice fishing in twenty-below zero temperatures. "You're insane," I told them. One replied, "No, we're having fun, you're the one insane for working when it's this cold." He was right. I went home.

.The early snowmobiles were prone to break down. I went up to Rio Grande Reservoir to check fishermen and my snowmobile wouldn't start. Ralph Conkey the caretaker of the dam, cranked up his

Rotary plow on Hwy 149 at Freemon Ranch   circa 1979

snowmobile, tied a rope to it, and pulled me on my cross-country skis. I swooped in on them, let go of the rope, glided up to them and checked their licenses and fish. They weren't surprised to see me. Who else but a game warden would pull such a stunt? I had

Patrolling by snowmobile

to maintain my image of showing up in unexpected ways

The morning it was 54 below zero Bob Wardell, the Mineral County Judge, walked into Ivan Weaver's drug store where men were huddled for coffee. He announced, "I was just down by the airport and I saw fourteen jackrabbits pushing a coyote to get him started." We needed laughter that warmed our souls that cold morning.

Nature has equipped wildlife with thick winter coats and the instincts to survive. God gave us intelligence either to move south as snow birds, or to adapt to a long, cold, and snowbound winter. To get around the district I installed studded snow tires on my four-wheel drive state truck. I also carried tire chains. We all had electric engine heaters for our vehicles and used synthetic lubricates in gear boxes and differentials.

Volunteers unload semi load of hay circa 1979

In early December temperatures briefly warmed and an incoming storm dumped rain on top of three feet of snow. When the cold temperatures returned, the snow turned to ice that locked the kitchen door, so to speak. Additional snowfall began to create a "Perfect Storm." Charles Steele, an area rancher, found blood on the snow where elk were slicing their legs pawing for something to eat. Winter wasn't even on the calendar yet and I knew we were in for a long siege.

Clayton Wetherill, Area Supervisor, Regional Manager Bob Rosette, and I made a plan. We knew that there would be a public outcry to feed the elk. I'd overheard a conversation at the post office suggesting that the Creede people would have to take control once again and feed the elk. As part of our plan, I wrote a local press release that the Division was going to feed elk and that we would need volunteers and community support. Over a hundred citizens signed up as soon as the word got out.

Clayton got bids for hay from Valley farmers. He ordered fifteen tons of the newly formulated elk pellet. Paul Hosselkus, the Mineral County Road Supervisor, had his crew bulldoze the snow for feed grounds on several ranches where elk were already concentrated. When we got word that a semi load of hay was on its way to Creede, Beth called volunteers to unload the hay. Temperatures remained below zero day after day for weeks. In bone chilling Temperatures men stacked a semi load of hay. Beth made hot chocolate for them. All winter long every Saturday morning volunteers hauled hay and pellets

Elk come off Long Ridge to feed where Charles, Billy and Kenny Dabney scattered hay. Bristolhead Mtn. on the horizon circa 1979

to feed grounds. Other volunteers scattered the feed during the week.

The operation was just getting started and running smoothly when the Division Director Jack Grieb called. He started chewing me out for writing a press release for our local newspaper detailing the feeding operation. My press release was picked up by Associated Press and went statewide. It was causing some public relations problems for the Division. The public was making an emotional demand that the Division feed elk and deer statewide. Grieb told me that it was okay to use the term "baiting" as in scattering hay to attract the animals to areas where there was natural forage. Unlike some areas of Colorado, there were no places in the Upper Rio Grande where elk could find anything to eat and the people knew it. I invited Grieb to come to Creede and personally observe the conditions. I had been using a helicopter to drop hay to some elk that snowmobilers had found marooned high on East Bellows Creek. We had begun baiting that herd down to a feed ground on the LaGarita Ranch. I took Grieb for an aerial tour of the feeding grounds. After his inspection he said, "You have a good FEEDING (emphasis added) operation going here. Keep up the good work."

When the snow finally started melting in late April everyone was relieved. The feeding operation was finished. We had fed well over a thousand head of elk. Just how much good did we accomplish? George Wiggins, Forest Service Biologist, and I organized a mortality transect to evaluate the Farmers Creek drainage. Local outfitters furnished horses for about a dozen students from the Creede High School. They rode to the upper reaches of the winter range. After some instruction the students lined up and hiked down the mountainside looking for carcasses. When they reached the Rio Grande River we tallied the count. The outfitters had prepared a lunch. The information we gathered was valuable and the kids made memories.

In spite of a hundred volunteers distributing three-hundred tons of hay and fifteen tons of pellets, I estimated that about fifty percent of the calves and nearly twenty-five percent of the adults died, but a little higher mortality than normal for a hard winter. Had we not fed the elk however, I believe the mortality would have been so severe that it would have taken several years to recover. The next few winters were not as severe and after reducing the cow elk harvest for a couple years, the elk population recovered. I was glad to see spring. I'd hardly had a day off all winter.

The Upper Rio Grande has marginal deer habitat. There are no significant browse species to sustain many deer. During a series of mild winters the deer population does well, but as soon as a severe winter occurs, that population will crash. Hunting or feeding plays no long term role in the management of deer in the Upper Rio Grande. With chronic wasting disease present in some Colorado deer herds, concentrating them by feeding them in the winter could foster the spread of this disease.

By the spring of 1979 the Division had spent its budget on feeding operations. The state entered a new fiscal year on July first. During that spring our field activities were greatly restricted until the legislature passed an emergency supplemental funding bill from the Game Cash Fund.

There have been several harsh winters and we applied what we learned from that 78-79 winter. We had no ration that deer could digest until the Division research section and the Colorado State University Wildlife Cooperative Research Center developed a ration that deer could digest. Those deer pellets were used successfully in the Gunnison basin during another severe winter in 1984.

There is a fine line between biological and political decision making. It is a dichotomy that agencies such as the National Park Service, Forest Service and state wildlife agencies preach to the public "Don't feed the animals," because feeding makes wildlife dependent on humans and less able to fend for themselves. Cold and hungry looking animals will always tug at our hearts. The emotional and economic demand to feed wild animals will always exist and it will always be a two-edged sword.

-50 low temp

high temp -20

A maximum/minimum thermometer on our front porch. Circa 1979

CHAPTER 12
Hunting seasons

The week before hunting season officers were busy answering phone calls from hunters who were sitting around their kitchen tables and firing off one question after another to plan their upcoming hunting trip. In most cases it was fun to be a part of their hunt. As the opening day approached, the intensity of the excitement reached a fevered level similar to when Colorado had an opening day for fishing season, like Christmas eve for a little boy anticipating Christmas morning, or like for a teacher the day before school starts. For many years the Division took advantage of referring hunters to our personal telephone phone numbers. The phone rang constantly.

If you like to hunt and fish then being a wildlife officer has to be the best job ever created . . . yeah-right. The truth is that when the fishing and hunting are at their best, a wildlife officer is at his or her busiest. When I went to work, Division employees were not allowed to hunt the first ten days of the deer and elk season, which was nineteen days long. When Jack Grieb became director he dropped that policy when multiple shorter seasons were implemented.

I made a decision to take our son Ralph elk hunting when he reached his fourteenth birthday. We hunted on an opening morning when I should have been working, but spending that time with him and showing him that he was a priority was as important to him as it was to me. We didn't get an elk that season, but there were more opportunities to come when he killed his first elk and later when we took up archery hunting and he killed an elk with his bow. We made some good memories.

I enjoyed working the hunting seasons. So many echoes reverberate in my mind of beautiful days on the trail as well as bitter cold, scary situations with nature and man. I met many good sportsmen and seldom had serious problems. Like all wildlife officers, I made my presence known in as many places I could, but effectively patrolling so much wilderness and roadless county is more than one officer can handle. There were seven other districts that surrounded the Upper Rio Grande. We were all overwhelmed by the work load, but we did what we could.

To increase our effectiveness the Division and the Rio Grande National Forest Service worked out an agreement with the Federal and District Attorneys so that officers of each agency could write citations in either jurisdiction. Phil Leggitt, the Mineral County

Sheriff and his deputies helped me during hunting season.   We
all met before the hunting season to plan our patrols. By then we
had two-way radio communication between our agencies.   Hunters
felt our presence throughout the district. We never found it
necessary to write citations outside our normal jurisdictions, but
summoned one another by radio to respond to violations.

I worked alone most of the time. The weather conditions
dictated whether the elk and deer would be in the high country or on
their winter range. Whenever feasible I worked in areas where I
thought I was least expected. I checked hunters wherever I found
them. If no one was in camp I left my business card in the handle of
the coffee pot so they knew I visited their camp. Most hunters
welcomed me and sometimes gave me information about any
suspicious activities. Over the years I developed many friendships.
Every fall I looked forward to seeing most returning hunting camps,
but then there were some that I wished would stay away.

Hunting hunters

The Denver law enforcement section sent me information that
two men in a party of four from New York State were going to be
hunting during the muzzleloader elk season with high powered rifles.
They were supposed to hunt somewhere near Bristolhead Mountain
west of Creede. I was instructed me to forego a case if it would
reveal that I was working on information provided by an informant.

In preparation to do some undercover work I grew a beard.
Because I knew the "who, what, when, and where" of a likely crime;
I planned to get into the area posing as an archery hunter and catch
these poachers. Larry Osborne, a Texas Game Warden buddy, was
joining me for an archery hunt. I told him we had to hunt some
hunters before we could go elk hunting.

The day before the season we drove Larry's Jeep into the area
looking for a truck with New York license plates. We wore
camouflage outfits, face paint, and took our archery equipment with
us. I packed my ticket book. We bypassed two muzzleloader
hunters who were hunting a day before the season in the head of
Shallow Creek, because we were looking for a truck with New York
license plates. Just before dark we set up camp.

High power rifle shots off in the distance awakened us at
daylight. We broke camp and drove around the head of Shallow
Creek toward the direction where the shots came from. We drove

to the top of Bristolhead Mountain at 12,706 feet and looked around. From high on the mountain I spotted a pickup truck and camp hidden off the trail that we had driven past. With our binoculars we could see two men walking into the alpine willows and carrying something back to their camp. They made a couple trips. At that distance we couldn't see exactly what they were doing, but we suspected they had an elk down. Why else would they be making trips out into the willows? So we drove down to the timberline and parked near their truck. It had New York license plates-BINGO! Thank you God!

We took our bows and "wandered" into their camp. They had killed a nice six-point bull elk and already had it quartered and hung up. I saw their high powered rifles leaning up against a log. When they saw us, one of them threw a jacket over the rifles. We played the role of two bow hunters and gave them the impression we were really impressed with their kill. I commented that it was archery and muzzleloader season and that I saw their high powered r i f l e s . One asked where we were from and Larry answered in his Texas drawl, "Texas."

One of them explained: "I don't know if you know it or not but this is grizzly country. We killed this elk with our muzzleloaders and went back to our truck and brought our high powered rifles to protect the meat. A muzzleloader just won't stop a grizzly. It is a felony to waste meat and we were only going to protect the meat so we wouldn't get into trouble." I struggled to keep a straight face.

I said, "I just come up here to go bow hunting with my buddy and walk into a violation like this and I am not going to walk away from it."

"What's it to you buddy?" he asked sarcastically.

"Well," I said as I got between them and their rifles, "I am Glen Hinshaw, District Wildlife Manager for the Colorado Division of Wildlife. That means Game Warden to you . . . Buddy!"

One of them said, "You can't prove we killed it with a rifle." I walked over to the elk while Larry kept an eye on them. Larry felt naked without his service revolver. I had my sidearm under my camouflage. I looked at a front shoulder and there was a bullet fragment with a piece of copper the size of a contact lens glistening in the early morning sun. Thanks again God! The copper jacket stuck to my finger tip. Muzzleloader bullets do not have copper jackets. I held it out to their view and said, "You are both under arrest for illegally killing this elk."

I took their rifles and walked them back to their truck.   I told them they had two choices. I would take them to jail and they could post bond or I could issue them Penalty Assessments (PAs) that they could pay on the spot and I would give them state-issued receipts. They talked it over and agreed to pay the PAs. They each paid $425 for their dastardly deed. They said they would have to borrow some extra cash from their two other buddies gear that was in their truck. Their partners apparently didn't know these two were going to do this. I asked them where their buddies were and one said they were camped over in Shallow Creek. I suspected that they were the ones we had seen the day before.

I returned their rifles, because the case was closed. As Larry and I pulled away with their elk, one asked if they could keep the antlers since they had traveled so far and had paid such a steep fin e . I threw them the heart and liver for their culinary enjoyment.

We drove back to Shallow Creek. I knew where there was an old sheep herder's shack and we hiked down and walked right into their camp. They didn't know anything about their buddies hunting with rifles, but I told them I had seen them hunting before the season. They each paid PAs for hunting out of season.

It was late afternoon as we bounced down the jeep trail (this was before a logging road was built into the area) toward North Clear Creek Falls. Larry said, "Well, there went a day of bow hunting." I replied, "Tell me you didn't enjoy catching those guys." He smiled. Doesn't matter who you are, it is very satisfying to catch poachers in the act.

The Pole Mountain Patrol

Early fall weather in the San Juans can be mild, dry and pleasant or cold, wet, and miserable-all in the same day. When the weather was mild I often worked the opening weekend horseback.   I requested the use of the regional airplane a couple days before the season to spot isolated hunting camps to decide where I could best spend my efforts. One season I decided to take a long ride around 13,716 foot Pole Mountain, skirt the headwaters of the Upper Rio Grande and into the Ute Creek Basin for a planned three day patrol. This roadless area was excellent elk country with a good number of hunting camps. Bob Clark, regional biologist, arranged for Don Masden, a temporary employee to ride with me. Don was raised on a ranch. Although I usually worked alone, I felt safer having someone to ride with me, especially an experienced horseman like Don.

We packed lite with a small tent, sleeping bags, food, and other necessities in our saddle packs and started up Lost Trail Creek above the Rio Grande Reservoir. The weather changed on opening morning. It was snowing lightly and conditions were ideal for elk hunting. We checked hunters and camps along the trail. All the hunters were properly licensed, but I wrote a couple for failure to wear fluorescent blaze orange.

We met some panic stricken Floridian hunters hurriedly coming down the trail. They were afraid of the snow and were heading back to Florida post haste. Elk hunters who are afraid of the snow have picked the wrong sport. Still, snow and winter conditions are to be reckoned with as Don and I were about to experience. We didn't know that we were riding into the face of a major snowstorm.

When we got to the pass between West Lost Trail Creek and the East Fork of Pole Creek at 12,000 feet, the falling and blowing snow reduced visibility to near zero. I thought of turning back, but if we could just make it to the Divide and the Colorado Trail we could descend down East Pole Creek and we'd be okay.

Paul Koretko, a Forest Service radio technician (and a high school classmate of mine) and Bud Wilshaw [sic] erected a solar powered electronic site on top of Bristolhead Mountain in 1969 that gave the Forest Service the only two-way radio communication that effectively covered much of the Upper Rio Grande.

I borrowed one of their pack sets during the hunting seasons. I was able to call out to the Creede office and told Betsy Rogers, the district clerk, of our location and intention to continue our patrol. Pilot error causes airplane crashes and a poor decision in the wilderness can become a fatal

Talking on the packset to Betsy Rogers during a whiteout

mistake as well. We made it to the Divide, but the snow was so deep that we couldn't find the Colorado Trail. I knew if we got too far to the left we would end up in an alpine bog that wasn't frozen hard yet, and if we got too far to the right there were the cliffs above Cataract Lake. Gene Bassett taught me, "Always trust your horse." I gave Diamond his lead and he slowly picked his way down country. As we got down to the timberline the visibility improved and we found the trail. As afternoon faded to evening we got to the junction of Pole Creek and the Rio Grande. We were cold, and tired after riding twenty tough miles. Diamond and Pet were just as tired.

The John Harrison camp from Amarillo, Texas welcomed us. I had become acquainted with them when one of their companions was killed in an avalanche in 1971. They had camped there for years. They unpacked and stored our gear, curried our horses, and shared grain and hay that they had for their own horses. Their custom made tent accommodated eight hunters with room to spare. The wood burning stove warmed the tent to equal their hospitality. Don and I downed a couple bowls of hot and spicy squirrel stew that they had brought from Texas. We had planned to pitch our tent, but they insisted we stay with them. We enjoyed a great evening of fellowship. Sleep came easy. Most hunting camps were hospitable to a visiting wildlife officer. I learned which camps had the best cooks. I've eaten spicy chili so hot it couldn't be frozen and coffee so thick it would float a horseshoe, but the fellowship and friendship I experienced was rich.

The morning broke and it was a winter wonderland of snow on the mountains. Don and I rode up the Bear Creek jeep road, checking hunters along the way. When we got to the ghost town of Beartown we took the trail up Starvation

Don Masden on Ute Pass
Weminuche Wilderness

Gulch and climbed through the snow above timberline, over Ute Pass and into the Ute Creek Basin

We rode past the spot where "Ernie" Wilkinson killed what was probably the last grizzly bear in the Upper Rio Grande in 1951. It was killing sheep. Along the way we surprised a few hunters. By late afternoon we were below the snow line near the forks of Ute Creek. We set up camp and ate the supper we had planned on eating the night before-steak, wild rice, and sautéed mushrooms. Pet and Diamond ate their fill of grass and grain.

The cold temperatures that come with clearing skies after a winter storm quickly penetrated our nylon tent. After we tucked the horses in for the night we turned in. Two candle lanterns soon warmed our cozy tent. When we crawled into our sleeping bags and blew out the candles the cold set in. It was quiet, unlike what it had been like for Beth the past couple of days and nights answering one phone call after another and building a stack of "While You Were Out" phone messages that I'd have to answer as soon as I got home.

I slept warm in my sleeping bag that was rated to 30 degrees below zero, but getting out of a cozy sleeping bag on a bitter cold morning is never pleasant. You gotta get up, pull on cold clothes, frozen boots and answer the call. Before you proceed you put the horses out to graze. Sometimes a campfire is more trouble than it's worth. We broke camp, saddled up and hit the trail. We made a lot of contacts and our being out amongst the hunters made them think twice about violating the law. Having a law enforcement presence may keep hunters in line, but most of them obey the hunting regulations and insist that others do as well. Don was good company on the trail and became a good friend. He followed his dream to become a District Wildlife Manager and later a big game biologist. Some of us just have the outdoor life in our blood.

It's a small world

One opening day I patrolled North Clear Creek near Heart Lake. It was a clear and crisp morning. I always wore a bright fluorescent blaze orange vest and a covering on the crown of my Stetson. I tied orange stringers on the bridle and Pet's tail. I could hardly sneak up on anyone. At a distance I looked like any other hunter. I rode up to my first hunter of the morning and checked his license and throughout that day I found everyone licensed and obeying the law.

The following year it snowed before the hunting season and elk were already down on their winter ranges. I had heard from a rancher that about 300 head of elk were on Long Ridge, a seven mile long grassy ridge below Bristolhead Mountain. There was no road so the only way I could work the ridge was horseback. It was snowing and the clouds were at ground level as I got to the top of the ridge at dawn. Some hunters had hiked onto the ridge in the dark. I looked a few yards in front of me and there was my first hunter all decked out in his blaze orange. As I approached him, he seemed a little shaken by my presence. "You again?" he exclaimed. He was the same guy I had checked a year before on opening day over by Heart Lake! He probably thought I was stalking him. A herd of elk came thundering by, but the clouds were so thick we never saw them.

I rode farther up the ridge and came upon two more hunters. As I dismounted, a herd of cows and calves came over the ridge right in front of us. I offered to hold their horses. There were no bulls in the herd. After the elk were out of sight one of the hunters said, "I suppose you want to check our licenses?" Since it was snowing, I was wearing a yellow saddle slicker and blaze orange. I asked, "What makes you think I want to check your licenses?" To which he replied, "Who else would

Checking a successful hunter in a snow storm on Long Ridge

be up here in this weather, without a rifle, and offer to hold our horses, but a game warden?" I checked more than a dozen bulls off Long Ridge that day.

When I contacted people I never knew what the long term effect might be, but once in a while I did learn about the difference a contact made. In 1969 I contacted three young men from Silverton with three nice bucks at West Ute Lake during an early buck season in the wilderness. They had failed to tag their deer and I wrote them citations, but I let them keep their trophy bucks. I took a picture of them with their deer for evidence. When the pictures came back from the developer, I sent a print to one of the boys.

Twenty-five years later I was checking hunters in the Disappointment Valley south of Norwood. I went into a camp of hunters who happened to be from Silverton. One of them asked me, "Did you used to be the game warden in Creede? I answered, "Yes." He said, "When I was a teenager you gave me a ticket for failure to tag my buck up at West Ute Lake. I still have the picture you sent me on my desk. We didn't know a game warden could be nice. We've tagged every deer since then."

That same season I was checking hunters on the Uncompahgre Plateau west of Montrose. I drove down a jeep road and saw a hunter standing a short distance from the road. I walked over to him and as I was checking his license he asked, "Did you ever work in the Weminuche Wilderness?" I answered, "Yes." He was flabbergasted, "You must work the whole state. You checked me fishing on Rincon LaOsa Creek." It had been about fifteen years since Dave Kenvin and I checked him about twenty miles deep into the Weminuche Wilderness. He had a license and everything was fine. Some people would call these coincidences. I don't believe in coincidence.

I didn't have the heart to wake him up

When any wildlife officer patrols a hunting season in Colorado he/she checks for a proper license, blaze orange garments, legal firearm, and for loaded rifles in a motorized vehicle. One morning I was checking hunters along the Divide west of Spring Creek Pass. As I came up the jeep road I saw a hunter decked out in blaze orange sitting against a big spruce tree. I parked about a hundred yards away and walked over to him. He was sound asleep. Rather than wake him up, I felt a little mischievous. Why can't a game warden have some fun once in a while? Instead of waking him up, I carefully placed my business card in the trigger guard of his rifle. I quietly returned to my truck and left without making contact. I still wish I'd stayed long enough to see him wake up and discover my calling card. It gave him something to talk about. He knew I was there.

The Piedra blizzard

I had received a report of hunters hunting the day before the opening day the previous year near Piedra Peak. There were some camps in that area that Larry Robinson, the District Forest Ranger, wanted to check. We prepared for a three day horseback patrol to circle a large area of the Weminuche Wilderness Area.

We didn't have ready access to local weather forecasts from either radio or television stations in Creede. Once again, we rode into another snowstorm. The day before the season opened we caught the trail from Copper Creek and rode south toward the Divide trail at Palomino Mountain. We were above timberline when the first snow squall hit us broadside. Wind driven snow plastered us. It was evening when we rode down to the Division's cabin near the Piedra transmountain water diversion. The single room log cabin was just a few yards from the Divide Trail, sheltered by tall spruce, next to a small meadow for the horses to graze.

As we rode up to the cabin there was a hunter with a rifle in one hand and the door padlock in the other. He heard our horses and looked up rather surprised. I could understand the temptation to shoot the lock to get into the cabin. It was snowing and their packer hadn't arrived with his party's camping gear. His hunting companions were standing around a fire across the creek trying to stay warm as the snow began to pile up. We were wearing saddle slickers, so he didn't know who we were. I identified myself and Larry. That really shook him up. I told him that they could come over to the cabin after we got the place opened up, the fire going, and our horses taken care of. Their packer showed up with their equipment and they were soon setting up camp.

Most backwoods cabins had been unlocked for years. Anyone could stay in the cabin and it was the code of the west to replace the firewood that you burned. The cabin was kept clean and ready for the next person. That culture gradually changed as wilderness travelers stole everything that wasn't bolted down and often trashed the cabin. The Division had to attach heavy window shutters and a door panel to prevent theft and vandalism.

The wood burning cook stove soon radiated heat and we began to warm up and be comfortable. The glow of the gas lantern added light and heat to the cabin. We cooked our supper and were soon settled in for the night. It was cozy inside the cabin while the snowstorm howled across the Divide. The trees and cabin protected the horses from the storm's blast. Larry and I enjoyed an evening of fellowship. I wondered how miserable those hunters were, but I knew they had a dry and comfortable camp. I didn't feel sorry for them, after all they were recreating and we were working.

The next morning I opened the door and was greeted with a foot of fresh snow, and it was still snowing and drifting. I knew there was no way we could continue our patrol over South River Peak as we had planned. It was urgent that we get out of the high country. I believe elk sense weather changes and will move overnight to lower country and the hunters would be moving with the elk. We closed the cabin. Our horses were ready to head down country. We saddled up and leaned into the wind driven snow as we rode down Red Mountain Creek to the Ivy Creek Campground. I think it is one of those "Murphy's Law" things that when it's cold and snowing the wind always blows in your face. Once again, the weather changed our plans.

The Grouse Park case

Ed Wintz, manager of the 4UR Ranch, was guiding a hunter one morning and as they were watching a herd of elk grazing in Grouse Park a volley of two dozen shots rang out. Six cow elk fell dead. Two hunters ran out from the timber. Party hunting, that is shooting an animal for someone else, was illegal. Ed rode down to the park and confronted the suspects. He did not leave until they had gutted the elk. These two men had no idea how even the thought of wasting game riled Creede people. In disgust Ed and his hunter rode back to the ranch and called me. He gave me a description of the hunters and where he thought they were camped. I drove to the head of Lime Creek and located two hunters that matched Ed's description. They had two legally tagged cow elk and denied being involved in the shooting in Grouse Park.

I radioed to Sheriff Harry Larson to have Ed meet me to identify the hunters. I took them off the mountain and Ed identified them as the shooters. I seized their rifles and wrote them summons for unlawfully killing four elk. The following day Ed and I took horses to the scene to gather evidence. The elk carcasses were gone. I put the Adams County Sheriff's training to good use and photographed the scene, the gut piles, and twenty-five empty cartridges. I took their rifles and the cartridge cases to the Colorado Bureau of Investigation (CBI) office in Pueblo. Ballistic tests by a Forensic Investigator matched the cartridges with their rifles. It was an open and shut case. Their defense attorney bargained with the District Attorney to charge one man who pled guilty for the illegal killing of four elk. At trial I presented my evidence of photographs and the CBI report. Ed didn't have to testify. The attorney didn't present any defense and the judge fined the defendant $1,600, which was the maximum fine and a lot of money in 1967.

A couple years later I was checking hunters in that area and found that same camp. A young man walked out to greet me and said that they had banned the men who killed those elk in Grouse Park and that they had cleaned up their act. He offered his hand shake and welcomed me into their camp. I may be gullible to trust people, but I believed him and never had another report of any wildlife violations related to that camp.

Navajo Sam?

Jim Houston, Gunnison Area Supervisor, got a report from two bighorn sheep hunters who saw two men kill a rocky mountain goat on Stewart Peak in the LaGarita Wilderness. We didn't even know there were any goats in that area. Jim asked if I could help him get into the area as it was closer from the Creede side of the Divide.

The next morning we took off horseback up West Willow Creek and over the Divide to Cascade Creek. The informants gave Jim good descriptions of the suspects and the location of their camp. Phil Mason was closing in from the Gunnison side. As Jim and I came down from the timberline we spotted them in their camp. We tied our horses and sneaked up on them. I got around behind them and Jim made a direct approach. He identified us as wildlife officers and I stepped out from behind a tree.

Jim said, "You know why we are here." The long-haired scruffy looking man replied, "You think I'm Navajo Sam." He did fit a description that we had for Navajo Sam, a nick name given to a man who had been robbing backpackers in the San Juan Mountains that summer. Jim said, "No, we know you killed a rocky mountain goat and you are going to take us to it." I patted them down for knives and unloaded their rifles. The two were cooperative and said they would take us to the goat.

We rode horses part way and then had to hike up a game trail to timberline. I looked up and here came Phil Mason with a quarter of a goat on his shoulder. We proceeded up the mountain to retrieve the rest of the goat which had been expertly skinned. When I asked them why they killed a goat, one replied that they ran out of food and got hungry.

We got back to their camp at sundown. Jim and I weren't prepared to spend the night. We made them break camp and headed back over the Divide

There was no moonlight and in the darkness I couldn't tell for sure where we were. I gave Diamond his lead. A horse has better night vision than a human and turning on a flashlight would only blind him. We just kept riding down West Willow Creek. Then, Diamond stopped. I couldn't see a thing, so I turned my little flashlight on and there was my horse trailer. "Good Boy!" I gave old Diamond a hug. Cowboys do that you know.

The next morning I wrote their citations. When I asked the one man for his occupation, he hesitantly answered, "Taxidermist." Judge Wardell fined them $1000. I gave the meat to the senior citizen lunch program. That old goat was so tough that no means of tenderizing could have made it more edible and it was like chewing rubber marbles.

The most conscientious hunter I ever met

A hunter called me at home and asked to meet with me. He introduced himself and we shook hands. Then he said, "I want you to give me a ticket. I killed a calf elk." He continued to say that he shot and killed a cow elk for which he had a license. He dressed the animal and went back to get help to pack it out. When they returned they found a calf elk dead lying next to the cow. The calf was already spoiled. He said that his wife had a cow license, but that putting her tag on it wouldn't make it right. There was no one else around. I had never seen anyone so distraught. Having had a similar experience with a hunter when I was in Cortez, I probed a little deeper. I told him that the fine for killing an elk was $400. He responded, "That is a cheap price to clear one's conscience." I asked him if he had proof that he killed the elk and he said no, but he would plead guilty. I knew Judge Wardell would probably throw me out of his courtroom if I brought this man before him.

I sensed a special connection with the man and asked him, "Are you a Christian?" and he answered "Yes." I asked him if he had prayed about his decision and he answered that he did. I asked, "Do you think God has forgiven you?" and he answered, "Yes." I said, "If God has forgiven you then the State of Colorado has nothing against you." I told him that if his conscience was still bothering him that he could make a donation to Operation Game Thief, the Division's poacher hotline. I found out later that he indeed had sent a $400 donation.

Not every hunter who turned himself in was turned loose. Such was the case one day when a hunter drove up to our house all

covered in blood. He said, "I killed elk, oh boy did I kill   elk."
He said that he had killed six elk by mistake. He admitted to
shooting into a herd of elk about six hundred yards away with a .270
rifle. When he shot, nothing dropped so he kept shooting until the
herd was out of sight. When he followed up his shots he found six
dead elk. I must admit either he was exaggerating or he was an
unbelievably good shot. Any hunter knows that is too far to be
shooting at anything at that distance. He killed the elk in Wason
Park west of the Wheeler Geological Area.

He promised to pack the animals out and just wanted me to
know, thinking I would not give him a ticket. We were still talking
when Rod Wintz came down the road in a cloud of dust. Rod, like
his brother Ed that I wrote about earlier, was pretty cool, but when I
saw the look on his face I knew there was more to the story. Rod
caught the guy in the act and it was a case of reckless and willful
destruction of wildlife. Since the elk had not been wasted, I didn't
have a felony case for willful destruction. That may have been,
because Rod confronted him. I wrote the violator a summons to
court and when he appeared, Judge Wardell fined him $2,400. The
Wildlife Commission suspended his hunting privileges in Colorado
for two years. Later I received information that he had done this
before and bragged about it.

The long arm of the law

I was driving up a jeep road on Shallow Creek checking hunting
camps. One camp had two properly tagged bull elk hanging. All of
the hunters had Colorado resident licenses and were from a front-
range city. But, one truck in the camp caught my eye. A personalized
Arkansas license plate read: "ELK". I asked who the truck belonged
to and one of them said the owner was out hunting. I drove on up
the road and checked more camps. When I returned a couple hours
later, the camp was gone. A hunter from a nearby camp waved
me down and told me that as soon as I had gotten out of sight, they
literally threw their tents and camp into their trucks and hurriedly
left.

I radioed the dispatcher run the "ELK" tag and it came back
registered to one of the hunters whose Colorado tag was on one of
the bulls. I called for an APB to have the vehicle stopped, but he got
out of state. He had used his son's address to obtain a Colorado
driver's license so he could buy a resident hunting license which was
cheaper than a nonresident license.

He lived near Fayetteville, Arkansas. I called the Arkansas Game and Fish Commission and they put me into contact with their wildlife officer in Fayetteville. He made an Arkansas residency check and gave me the evidence I needed. After a little police work, I called the hunter's son and told him that his dad was in big trouble for taking an illegal elk across state lines in violation of the federal Lacey Act, which carried huge fines. Without hesitation he gave me his dad's phone number.

I called his dad, identified myself, and it got so quiet on the other end of the line that even the chickens quit clucking. I told him that he could go one of two ways: state or federal wildlife charges. I sent him a citation for fraudulent purchase of a resident license and illegal possession of an elk. He paid it immediately. In the meantime the Arkansas wildlife officer further shook him up when he dropped by his residence and seized the elk, which was donated by his agency to dispose of at their discretion. An investigation is like putting a puzzle together when you don't know what the picture looks like. Eventually the evidence produces a satisfying result.

The long arm of the law worked on fishermen as well. A resort owner called Dave Kenvin to report some fish hogs. They were going to leave the next morning, so Dave and I set up a check station and waited for them to come through. We waited until mid-morning, but they didn't show up. Dave checked with his informant and our suspects had left for Texas about four o'clock in the morning.

I figured they might be going through Dalhart, Texas on their way home. The timing seemed good, so I called a Texas Game Warden buddy, Dick Byrne in Dalhart, and gave him the name and car license number. He called an hour later saying that as he drove through town he spotted the car at a convenience store. He walked up to the driver, called him by name and said, "A Colorado Game Warden asked me to count your fish." The man about choked. Dick said that he didn't think we wanted to extradite them for two fish over the limit, but he put the fear into them about violating the Lacey Act. They had a big fish fry the night before so they wouldn't be over the limit. The informant had chewed them out.

Colorado started an Interstate Wildlife Violation Compact with the state of Nevada in 1985 and as of 2013 included forty-two states. If a person violates a wildlife law in one state and ignores a summons, the state he lives in can punish him by suspending hunting and fishing privileges.

God didn't save the preacher

I was working an antelope season north of Villa Grove one fall. I watched a hunter kill an antelope, dress it out and load it into his pickup. He came down the road where I stopped him. He was very nervous. He had a valid antelope license for the area, but had failed to attach the carcass tag.

He used an old ploy to explain: "I forgot to tag the antelope and this is certainly not intentional. I am the minister of the gospel in a large church and I wouldn't lie to you. Since you and I are the only ones who know about this, would you just let me go and I won't say anything?"

I pointed to the sky and said, "HE knows." As I completed his citation I gave him one of my little sermons, "I am a brother in Christ. You are asking me to corrupt myself and to sin against God and the people of the State of Colorado." His reply, "Well, I wouldn't want to see you lose your salvation over this."

My final words were, "I appreciate your concern for my salvation. Press hard, there are five copies." Likewise, it didn't happen very often, but I deplored any law enforcement officer who flashed his badge and asked me to give him a professional courtesy by turning my back on his violation.

Stalked by an elk

An archery hunter hiked six miles from Ruby Lake to report someone hunting with a rifle during archery season. Early the next morning I saddled Diamond and rode into that area listening for rifle shots. I followed the trail from Ruby Lake over to Jumper Lake. As I was getting close to timberline a bull elk bugled. What an adrenaline rush it is to be close to such a magnificent wild animal. I had a bugle with me and gave it a toot. I reined Diamond and we listened.

A big six-point bull walked out of the timber about fifty yards from us. He was on the fight as he thrust his massive antlers into a wallow, threw sod into the air and bugled. I leaned forward in the saddle to reduce my silhouette. He snorted, bugled again, and started stalking us and lowering his head as if to charge.

Diamond was getting really nervous and I could feel his muscles tense. I held a tight grip on the saddle horn. Then he stopped about fifteen yards from us, shook his antlers, sniffed the air, turned, and silently disappeared into the timber.

Of course, wouldn't you know, I didn't take a camera   with me that day. I was proud of old Diamond for holding steady. I can see me now being chased by a bull elk and galloping through a hunting camp yelling, "You get this one and I'll go get another one!"

We continued our patrol, but by sundown I'd heard no shooting and all the archery hunters were hunting with bows. I checked several camps for firearms and found none. Still, the day was not a waste. Legitimate hunters were glad to see me and if I did contact the culprit, he knew I was looking for him. More importantly, he also knew that other archery hunters wouldn't tolerate shooting an elk with a rifle during the archery season.

A couple years later an informant sent me the name of a man who might be hunting with a rifle during the archery season in that same area between Ruby Lake and Texas Creek. Dave Kenvin and I rode from Squaw Creek into Little Squaw Creek and camped for the night. Bright and early the next morning we rode over to Texas Creek. We had no more than reached the Texas Creek Trail when our suspect came riding down the trail on his horse. He had a rifle in its scabbard and no bow.

We hadn't seen him actually hunting, so I called him by name and flat out told him we knew what he was doing. He had an archery license and equipment back at his camp. He denied he was hunting with a rifle and only carried it to protect himself against bears. To Dave and me that was a worn out excuse. We didn't have a case and had to let him go, but as with many contacts, he knew we were there.

Wally Shirra's close call

It was elk season, October 25, 1971 and I was taking a break at home. I was looking out our living room window toward the Creede airport about quarter of a mile away and suddenly a two engine plane crashed onto the runway, skidded to a stop, and burst into flames. I grabbed a fire extinguisher, ran to my truck, radioed for a fire truck, and sped to the end of the runway. When I got to the crash site the right engine was ablaze, but everyone got out of the plane safely.   I hit the flames with my extinguisher and nearly had the flames out when Paul Hosselkus arrived with a fire truck and he quickly finished extinguishing the fire.

I went over to check on the folks standing with Ad Britain, a local rancher. He said everyone was shaken up, but were okay. Ad introduced me to the man, his wife and daughter who had been elk hunting on his ranch. "Glen, I want you to meet Wally Schirra." We shook hands and under the circumstances I probably s a i d something stupid. Being dumfounded is usually a good excuse. Ad hosted a number of astronauts at his ranch over the years.

Wally Schirra was one of the original seven Mercury astronauts who also flew on the Gemni and Apollo space flights as the United States prepared for a flight to the moon. Schirra was an avid hunter. He rode with me back to the ranch where they made other arrangements to get home. One engine had failed on takeoff and at 9,000 feet above sea level such a plane could not take off and maintain flight with one engine. The experienced pilot wisely shut the plane down in time to safely crash land at the end of the runway. I met Schirra several more times at the Division's annual inservice training sessions when he presented the Wildlife Officer of the Year award on behalf of Shikar Safari Club an international sportsmen's association. Schirra experienced many exciting moments in his life, but one of his closest calls was At the Creede airport.

CHAPTER 13
There are bears out there

San Juan grizzlies?

Early trappers and explorers killed grizzly bears throughout Colorado. Pioneer ranchers trapped and shot grizzlies that were killing their cattle, sheep, and horses. The grizzly bear had been extirpated from Colorado except for the San Juan Mountains. The last known grizzly bear was killed in the Upper Rio Grande in Starvation Gulch by Federal Trapper Ernest Wilkinson in 1951. Lloyd Anderson, a federal trapper from Pagosa Springs had killed several grizzlies in his career; the last one in 1952 in the Pine River drainage. Anderson reported watching a grizzly sow and two cubs between Rock Lake and the Ute Creek Basin in 1967, but that sighting was not confirmed.

Fearing that the grizzly was extinct in Colorado, the Wildlife Commission established a grizzly bear refuge on both sides of the Divide between Vallecito and Rio Grande reservoirs between 1955 and 1965. Although there were other reports and searches for grizzly bears in the San Juans, none had produced evidence of their existence such as tracks, hair or pictures.

Hal Burdick, Southwest Regional Wildlife Biologist, initiated a grizzly bear search in 1970. We didn't have infrared cameras and high tech recorders then. The ground search concentrated in the San Juan Mountain Range from the headwaters of the Rio Grande to New Mexico. The Division purchased some horses destined for slaughter for grizzly bait. Biologists thought that only a grizzly bear would be large enough to move a horse carcass. A black bear or mountain lion might scavenge, but would be unable to move it

One summer morning I saddled Pet and led a horse over the Divide toward Sugarloaf Mountain between the East Fork of the Piedra River and Porphyr Gulch. I was a little apprehensive riding alone into such rugged country with no map and only general directions into historic grizzly country. Even Pet was more alert than her usual self. Her ears moved like a radar antenna toward every sound. Her nostrils flared to pick up the scent from any threat. The only sound of nature was a marmot whistling an alert to some grazing elk. I found an alpine meadow where a scavenging grizzly would likely leave tracks as evidence of its presence. Sadly, I drew my pistol and killed the horse in a place maybe more befitting him than a slaughter house. I tried to console myself with that thought. There is no joy in killing any animal.

Later, I flew with Gordon Saville, our regional pilot, to show him the location of the carcass so he and Hal could determine if the carcass had been moved. Follow-up visits would have been made if there was evidence of a carcass being moved. Hal placed a few remote cameras near other carcasses to increase the chances of documenting the bear's existence. Most of the pictures were of ravens, magpies and other scavengers and more black bears than we previously thought existed in the San Juans.

We found no evidence of grizzly bears, but any declaration that the grizzly was extinct in the San Juans was proven false in 1979 when outfitter Ed Wiseman was mauled by a grizzly on the Conejos River drainage in the South San Juan Wilderness Area. Ed killed the bear in self-defense. That incident sparked another fruitless search for the elusive grizzly. There have been reports, but no confirming evidence of their existence. If you are interested in further information about grizzlies in the San Juans I recommend the book *Ghost Grizzlies*, by David Petersen.

People have asked me if I think Colorado should reintroduce the grizzly bear to the state. In my opinion that would be a big mistake. In the past hundred years humans have so fragmented those habitats where grizzlies once lived that such an introduction of this mighty predator would cause unacceptable bear-human conflict, far beyond those caused by black bear encounters.

I would inject here as well, that the reintroduction of the wolf would cause even more conflict. There would be the consequence of a dramatic reduction in elk and deer populations similar to what has occurred in Montana, Idaho, and Wyoming. I believe an informed public would reject such a proposal. People who wouldn't have to live with these consequences may tend to favor such reintroductions as romantic and ecologically necessary, but those ranchers and others who live on the land would disagree. The legislature would decide if such reintroductions take place. Right now neither is under consideration for reintroduction.

Bears have people problems

Black bears live throughout most of Colorado. They even find their way into cities where wildlife officers respond to calls of panic, curiosity, and sincere care for the bear. These magnificent animals get into trouble when they trespass onto lands that people took from them. Thus it befalls the wildlife officer to deal with bears that are having people problems.

- "Come up to our cabin and see OUR cute little bear. We feed it dog food every day. He is so cute." At the end of summer however, these bear lovers quit feeding THEIR bear. Then the call came in, "Come up here and kill YOUR damn bear. He tore the screen door off its hinges and destroyed our barbeque grill and we want the state to pay for the damages."

- "We have a bear problem. A bear climbed into our station wagon through an open window, ate the head rests, and perforated the upholstery. I need your help to document my insurance claim. When the car was new we went to a track meet and when we returned to our car, we found that a discus had gone through the windshield and the insurance paid. Later we were at a resort in Missouri and someone opened the corral gate and a herd of horses stampeded between our cabin and the car. They caved in the side of the car. The insurance paid. But, this they ain't going to believe. Would you write a letter to my insurance agent explaining that a bear really did this?" I graciously wrote a letter for him.

- A caller from a mountain subdivision demanded, "Come up here quick and kill a bear!" I asked, "Has the bear hurt anyone or done any damage?" The caller answered, "Well no, but we can't have wild animals running around up here!" I gathered some homeowners together and tried to convince them to store their garbage and trash to remove the food source and the bear wouldn't return.

- Al Randall, the Creede city marshal, called me in the middle of the night: "A drunk just stumbled out of the bar and smack dab into a bear." I asked, "Is the bear okay?" He said that the bear was scared and climbed a power pole. I told him to leave the bear alone and direct the customers out the back door. The bear soon came down and ran back to the mountains.

- Some hippies camped at the end of the road up Miners Creek. They were trashing the place. I caught a nuisance bear in another area and released it just below their camp. The next day they abandoned their camp. When I told the

sheriff what I had done he said that he thought I had
been very cruel . . . to the bear.

• I got a call about a nuisance bear at a summer home group.
When I arrived the scared little bear was hanging to the
top of an aspen tree next to a house. A crowd had gathered
to see this little bruin. I borrowed a step ladder, got up on the
roof and crawled out to the gable where I was only a few feet
from the bear. A breeze was blowing toward him. Without
t h i n k i n g the whole thing through, I started spraying the
bear with MACE. It just looked at me, didn't even blink, and
wasn't irritated by the spray. We didn't have pepper spray
then. I looked down and the crowd was running away
coughing and rubbing their eyes

I discovered a new approach to handling a nuisance bear
complaint: MACE the people! I climbed down and told the
caretaker to leave the bear alone. By evening it descended from
its perch and went off into the woods.

I understand the frustration people have with bears. One bright
moonlight night we were sound asleep when Queenie, our German
Shepard, started barking. I looked out the bedroom window and
there was a bear in our trash can. After I let Queenie in the house, I
loaded my shotgun with five cracker shells, opened the window and
fired five quick rounds at the bear. The M-80s started exploding all
around the bear and it ran off and out of sight.

The next morning Rod Wintz called from the Wason Ranch
about half a mile down river. He said, "We had a bear visit the
ranch last night." I gave him a box of cracker shells for his 12 gauge
shotgun. The bear never returned, but Rod kept the cracker shells
just in case. Later that fall Rod took his dad duck hunting and
loaded his shotgun with "these new shells". When they jumped some
ducks his dad fired and when the cracker shells exploded, he
thought the ducks were shooting back at him.

Every wildlife officer or office receptionist could write a book
about the misconceptions that some people have about wildlife.
Most people want to be close to Mother Nature, but when it comes
right down to it, they are afraid of her. Since many do not know
how to cope with wild animals, they want them destroyed so that
they will feel safe.

Bearly management

Wild bears pretty much stay to themselves and are seldom seen or cause problems. It was apparent that our nuisance bear management system wasn't working. The primary technique for handling bear complaints was to live-trap the bear and relocate it to a place

Number 32 about ready to awaken

where we thought it wouldn't be a problem. Since there are bears throughout the Colorado Rockies it is a problem to relocate them where they don't get into trouble again. For example, I hauled nuisance bears to the top of Spring Creek Pass on the Divide and released them into the Lake City district. It wasn't until we started tagging nuisance bears that Phil Mason and I realized we were swapping bears.

I released one bear in what I thought was an isolated place near Pooltable Mountain, but after I released it I drove farther down the road with the bear trap in tow and I saw a sheep herder tending about 2,000 sheep. I

Releasing a nuisance bear on Spring Creek Pass

had just released my bear in the middle of his sheep allotment.

I didn't stop to visit that day. I was lucky that the bear never bothered his sheep.

Some bears became trap-wise and were difficult to catch. These "gourmet" bears were very picky. I had one bear at Santa Maria Reservoir that somehow learned how to eat the bait without pulling the trigger. I thought surely something was wrong with the trigger. I wisely had a friend go with me. I took some WD-40 and crawled into the trap - bad idea. I sprayed the trigger mechanism and it worked. I then experienced how a bear must feel when that steel door slams shut. I was sure glad to have a real friend to open the trap. Like a bear, I was in a poor position to negotiate my release.

I only had one other encounter with a wild bear when I was leading a pack train down the North Fork of the Pine River. I looked down the trail and a bear was walking towards us. He looked up and darted off into the timber. It happened so fast that the horses and the others with me didn't see the bear. It was not a good place to have a rodeo.

I investigated a report from a rancher that a bear had killed some sheep on Texas Creek. Dave Kenvin, Beth and I rode to the camp, which had been demolished by a bear. Coyotes had killed a couple sheep and a bear scavenged on the carcasses, but the state paid for the shredded tent.

A bear terrorized one sheep herder who was asleep in his trailer on Fischer Mountain, when his abode started rocking. A bear tore a piece of aluminum and ripped a hole in the corner of the trailer and was able to reach into the trailer. You can imagine the fear of seeing a bear's paw and claws thrashing about just a few feet from you as he searched for food. I trapped that bear and hauled him to the top of Spring Creek Pass.

A cook at the Wilderness Ranch was preparing breakfast in the kitchen lodge. Pancakes were on the menu. Just as the bowl of batter was ready, a bear walked through an open door into the kitchen. The cook was face to face with a hungry bear and so he let him have it, mixing bowl and batter in its face. The cook vaulted over a counter and out the door. A nearby rancher had a bear license and the season was open, so the bear was shot.

Very few people have encounters with bears, but as humans intrude into bear country, the conflicts will occur. After I left Creede the Division established a "Two Strikes and You're Out" policy. When a bear was recaptured a second time it was destroyed. Any peace officer is authorized to kill a bear that is a threat to human life for a first time offense. The Division's education program in conjunction with those of the U.S. Forest Service and National Park Service has probably saved more bears than any other program. More citizens know how to live and recreate in wild country with wildlife. Since that program started, some communities have adopted ordinances requiring bear proof garbage containers. There will always be conflicts with bears and other wildlife as we invade their habitat.

CHAPTER 14
Potpourri

When wildlife officers get together socially, the stories flow without chronology or continuity – a potpourri of miscellaneous sundry memories. Here's some of mine:

Yogi Bear cleans up poachers

Costilla County east of Alamosa, Colorado was a poaching hotbed. Deer came down from summer ranges in the Sangre De Christo Mountains to lower winter ranges. Poachers particularly favored the west side of LaVeta pass on U.S. Highway 160. One night Dick Weldon and I were watching a stretch of highway where hundreds of deer wintered. Harvey Bray, Area Supervisor and Officer Don Crane were hiding in the chase car.

Dick and I watched a car stop, turn it's headlights into an area where we knew there were deer and after a few moments, turned the lights off. In a few minutes the headlights came back on and the car drove away. This was a typical MO [Modus Operandi] for poachers who had just killed a deer. We radioed to Harvey and Don who chased the car down and found a deer in the back seat. They wrote the poachers citations and seized the deer.

They had just finished those citations when a full moon bathed the mountains with surreal light. It was a beautiful night to go poaching. It was so cold that we kept the truck heater running all night. Then another car stopped. A spotlight shined up the hillside, two shots rang out and a deer dropped to the ground. Two men hiked up to the deer while the driver turned around and drove up the highway.

I watched the car make a U turn and stop right in the middle of a curve on the highway with its lights off. Dick watched the two men gut the deer. Just as they were dragging the deer off the hill, a semi-truck entered into the field of view of my binoculars. WHAM! The semi sent the car flying into the borrow ditch. I watched in horror as the semi flipped onto its side and slid up the highway in a tremendous shower of sparks.

Dick radioed to Harvey and Don that there had been a crash. They raced up the highway and picked up the two poachers who were hiding behind some bushes and went on to the wreck to check on injuries. We called the State Patrol for an ambulance and a patrolman. Dick and I left our hiding place as fast as we could.

Don described the scene as they arrived:

"The semi was on its side blocking the highway. The truck driver was okay, but the driver of the car was lying in the barrow ditch, hurt, and not very responsive. The smell of diesel fuel permeated the night air. The trailer had ruptured and scattered its cargo of Yogi Bear Bubble Bath powder onto the highway. We gave the driver first aid until the ambulance arrived and took him to the hospital. That trip cost the poachers the deer, car, and a semi loaded with Yogi Bear Bubble Bath. That had to be one of the most expensive poaching trips anyone ever made. One of the poachers admitted that they had driven over a hundred miles from Rocky Ford to poach a deer." When will they ever learn?

The PR side of law enforcement

A standard approach to checking fishermen for any wildlife officer is to sneak up on the lake or river and observe who is "committing fish." Just by observing fishermen you can sometimes predict who has a fishing license or may be violating other fishing regulations. When I made a license check I always assumed the hunter or angler had the proper license. I never asked IF a person had a license, because he or she would immediately be defensive, because I appeared to doubt his or her integrity. Most officers contacted people this way. Violators on the other hand can't help but look guilty or act very nervous.

Colorado had a regulation that you could only fish with one fishing rod unless you had a second rod stamp. I watched one angler fishing with at least six fishing rods. I approached him and he wasn't the least bit nervous. He was a very friendly man from Louisiana enjoying his Colorado vacation. He was astonished when I told him that he was in violation of Colorado fishing regulations that allowed only one fishing rod. Back home he could use as many as he wanted. He hadn't read the fishing regulations. He asked me if I was going to throw him in jail. I didn't lecture him that it was his responsibility to know the law. Instead, I gave him a copy of the fishing regulations and told him that I was going to go around the lake and check all the other fishermen and when I got back to him I would give him a little test and if he passed my test, I wouldn't take him to jail or give him a ticket. When I got back to him, I'm sure he knew the fishing regulations better than anyone around the lake. To reward him I gave him a little coaching on how to catch trout and gave him one of my favorite flies that my dad invented called "Old Faithful" (best fly I ever used). I wished him good luck and we shook hands. I like a man with a firm handshake.

I was checking fishermen at Love Lake and approached a lady fumbling with her reel. I sat down by her and took the reel apart and untangled the line. She thanked me and cast her line out. Then she asked me, "I supposed you'd like to check my license?" I answered, "Well, since I'm here." As I wrote her name and license into my contact book she asked me, "Do you recognize my name?" I told her that the last name looked familiar. She proudly said, "I'm Mrs. Vanderhoof. My son is Governor John Vanderhoof. I smiled, shook her hand, and said, "I'm very pleased to meet you and please give my regards to the Governor." She said she'd put in a good word for me.

I was checking fishermen at Road Canyon Reservoir and saw a young boy fishing all alone. I saw that he was having trouble casting. His reel was all tangled up. I sat down with him and he told me that his dad and family were out in the boat and there wasn't room for him. They left him with a tangled reel and dried up salmon eggs for bait. After I got his line untangled, I asked a nearby fisherman for a couple worms. The boy made a good cast and I think the good Lord grabbed one of His fish and stuck it on the hook and the lad reeled it in. The boy beamed with pride and told me that it was his first fish. I took his picture.

When his dad and family trolled by in their boat, I waved him over to the bank and checked their licenses. I told his dad that he had missed out on being with his son when he caught his

A boy's first fish

first fish. I copied his address and when I got the pictures from the developer, I mailed the picture to the young lad. Some people think that law enforcement officers are just looking for violators, but most of us looked after people in a positive way. It made my day to make someone's day a little better.

Whenever possible I attempted to turn a negative into a positive. A case in point was the time I contacted a man and his son walking down a trail during deer   season.   The boy was carrying   a hunting rifle and had a hunting license. It was the young man's   first deer hunt. The father didn't have a rifle or a license. They had seen some deer, but didn't get o n e .   The dad was sporting a nasty   cut around his right eye; the size of the eyepiece of the rifle scope. He claimed he'd walked into a tree branch. It was obvious to me that he had taken the rifle, shot at a deer and when the rifle recoiled, it drove the scope into his face. I walked him to my truck and bandaged his wound.

I got him off to the side away from his son, and I told him t h a t I knew what had happened, because I had a rifle scope recoil into my face once. I really didn't have a case, but we had one of my little chats. I told him that he had robbed his son of his first chance at a deer. By his actions he implied that he didn't have confidence in his son and that his relationship with his son was less important than deer meat. It didn't matter if his son hit or missed the deer. It was more important that they were together sharing the experience. The man choked up, shook my hand, and thanked me. I've thought of them over the years and I hope that they have had a g o o d relationship and many memories of good hunts together.

Eyes like an eagle

Thieves and poachers prefer plying their trade in isolation and/or darkness. I spent many a night watching for spotlighters. A soaring eagle can spot its prey from high in the sky. Eagles don't fly at night, but we did. One night officers were stationed in strategic places around the Valley while pilot Jim Olterman and Clayton Wetherill looked down through the darkness for their prey; poachers shining telltale beams of light.

I got the call to scramble to an area southwest of Saguache. When I got close I turned my spotlight skyward and was immediately spotted. Clayton directed me through a maze o f logging roads into a well hidden hunting camp. Four hunters were standing around a campfire as I drove up. I kept my headlights pointed at them, stepped out of my truck, identified myself and said, "You boys were doing a little spotlighting tonight." They denied my accusation. One of them asked me what made me think they had been spotlighting. I pointed to the moonless sky above and they could hear the drone of our Cessna. "How else would I find your camp in the dark?" I asked. I searched their truck and found a powerful spotlight. However, their unloaded rifles were lying in the tent. They admitted they had indeed been spotlighting, hoping t o see some elk to hunt the next day. I had no case, but asked to check their hunting licenses. One of them had his wife's license. Another hunter accidentally handed me two licenses, one of them being that of a friend. I wrote them citations for misuse of licenses. The aerial patrol was never fruitless when we made contacts like that. The word got out and probably had some measure of deterrence.

Poacher coming your way

Another time officers were scattered across the east side of the Valley just before daylight. Tom Rauch and I were waiting at the mouth of a canyon. Gordon Saville, Clayton Wetherill and Forbes Trinchera Ranch biologist Rod Horn were in the Cessna patrolling for poachers. They spotted a pickup with an elk in the back. Tom and I got the call that the poachers were headed in our direction. The poachers spotted the low flying plane and pulled the elk out of the truck and fled down the road. When they came around a corner Tom and I had the road blocked. It was like having a fish driven into a net. They stopped and denied they had killed anything. They had no gun with them. We called for backup to arrest and transport them to jail. Clayton directed Tom and me to the elk carcass. We loaded the elk and slowly drove back down the snow covered road. I spotted a footprint in the snow next to our suspect's vehicle tracks. Tom walked out from the truck a few yards and found the suspect's rifle lying in the snow. We collected samples of fresh elk blood and hair from the bed of the truck. We had a solid case. The poacher got a lawyer, went to court and pleaded "not guilty". His lawyer tried for nearly a year to get the case dismissed, but when all his motions and hearings were exhausted, the defendant pleaded guilty, was fined, and the case closed.

Pay day pay off

One winter day I got a phone call that someone had poached an elk about six miles south of Creede on Highway 149. The snow was about two feet deep. Four quarters had been expertly carved off and the rest of the carcass abandoned. During my investigation I f o u n d a copy of a pay slip with a name and address lying in the bloody snow next to the carcass. A state snowplow driver reported that another elk had been poached just below Blue Creek. That elk also had its four neatly trimmed quarters missing. It was obvious that whoever did this knew the meat butchering business. The name on the pay slip had a Denver address.

I turned the case over to the Denver headquarters law enforcement section. Their investigation led them to the area west of what is now Sports Authority Field at Mile High Stadium. They were able to locate the culprit and write a ticket for killing elk out of season. Sure enough, he and his companions were meat cutters at one of the meat processing plants in the Denver area.

Yield not to temptation

I don't know where the original idea came from, but we started using decoy deer to catch spotlighters and road hunters. We placed a life-like Styrofoam dummy where approaching headlights would highlight the "deer". Two of us hid out of sight while other officers waited down the road for us to radio them to stop a suspect vehicle. We usually charged shooters for shooting from a public road or from a vehicle and sometimes for use of artificial light as an aid in hunting.

One night Area Supervisor Jerry Apker and I were hiding in some bushes when a truck came down the road and stopped with the headlights shining on the decoy. The driver got out, stood in the middle of the road, and drew a bead on the decoy, but he lowered his rifle and said, "I can't do it."

Usually we'd just let them go on down the road, but Jerry suddenly announced our presence and scared the pants off them. We caught a few violators, but most hunters were ethical even when they thought no one was looking. Anyone can be tempted and most hunters resisted the temptation

Check station ahead

When I checked fishermen while they were in the act of fishing, I seldom found anyone over the bag limit which for many years was ten trout. When the fishing was good the temptation to take an over bag limit of fish got some fishermen into trouble. Some people who fished for several days would smoke, can, or freeze more than their limits. To catch fish hogs we set up check stations to catch them leaving the area. Following constitutional guidelines we stopped traffic. Most travelers were just briefly stopped and continued on their journey.

One day we had a check station on the west side of Del Norte on U.S. Highway 160. Someone saw a truck hit his brakes and pull behind a filling station. One of the officers ran over to the station and saw the driver throwing bags of fish into a trash barrel. When the driver came into the check station, the officer followed him. We counted about a hundred fish over his limit.

The next day I was checking fishermen on the Rio Grande at 30-Mile Campground. A fisherman complained that the river was "fished out." I told him that the fishing had been good, because we caught a fisherman with about a hundred fish he caught from that stretch of river. He asked me if I could tell him the name of the fish hog and where he was from. I told him and he dropped his fishing rod and started jumping up and down like a cheerleader. His fishing buddy came to see what the cheering was all about.

"They caught Frank (not his real name)!" Both of them were ecstatic. Then he explained. "You caught one of the worst game hogs who does this all the time and brags about it." He asked me how much the fine was and I told him about five dollars a fish. He said, "Frank works for me and I've needed to ask someone to work overtime and now I know who to ask." The saddest part of this story was that "Frank" was teaching his young son to follow in his footsteps.

Brothers behind the badge

When I went to work there were no female law enforcement officers. It was a man's world until 1975 when Susan Smith became the first female Colorado District Wildlife Manager and we became brothers AND sisters behind the badge. Sheriffs, wildlife officers, town marshals, and state troopers were the only law enforcement presence in rural areas. Occasionally agents from the CBI and the FBI were called in for investigations. We worked together whenever called upon.

Creede was a community similar to the 1950s television show Mayberry, RFD. and Sheriff Harry Larson was more like Andy Griffith's character, Sheriff Andy Taylor. He was sheriff for twenty-eight years. I never saw Harry carry a gun. He knew everybody and everyone knew and respected him. Like any good lawman Harry managed most conflicts with his tongue.

Then one night Joe Stout, a businessman in South Fork, was murdered in his shop. Harry called me and asked me to help him set up a roadblock in case the suspect came our way. I strapped on my

.357 and took my 30-06. Harry was unarmed. We stood out on the highway and Harry flagged down oncoming motorists. We didn't have any idea who we were looking for. Fortunately for us Harry knew everyone coming up the highway, but if the suspect had come our way, he could have run over or shot both of us. Other lawmen have been killed doing what we did. The suspect was later apprehended.

Wildlife officers across the state were members of local law enforcement groups such as the San Luis Valley Peace Officers Association. We met monthly to share intelligence and the need for mutual support. FBI agents taught us firearm proficiency, officer survival, investigation and arrest techniques and the latest information on rules of criminal procedures. During the Vietnam protest era of the 1970s we learned how to support police doing riot control. Eventually, all Colorado Wildlife Officers completed the same training That all Colorado peace officers receive.

I thank God For radio dispatchers who

FBI agent Neil Fore instructs firearm proficiency to some Valley Peace Officers circa 1970

played a key role in law enforcement. When I was in Cortez the sheriff's wife was a dispatcher and when I went out-of- service at night, instead of saying 10-4, in a lilting voice she would say, "Good night." Phil's wife Diana dispatched for Mineral County and her 10-4 was, "Okie Dokie." The State Patrol dispatchers went by the numbers, but in small towns we didn't always follow the ten-code and it was never out of line for a dispatcher to relay a message that I'd be late home. All of them knew the country and kept track of us as best they could. They were our life lines. They did what they could to keep us safe.

I ran a 10-28 and '29 [wants and warrants] on a wildlife violator that I was suspicious of.   I knew something was wrong when the dispatcher came back to me, "What is your 10-20 '[location]. I told him and he said that there was an active warrant for the man. In case something went wrong, he knew where I was. I held the suspect until a deputy sheriff came and took him into custody. I never did know what the man was wanted for.

The Division had training sessions since the 1950s, but it wasn't until 1971 that Clyde Slonaker was assigned as the first full-time training officer. He established a six month training program for new officers. In addition to classroom instruction trainees were given month long assignments to work with district wildlife officers. Since there was such an emphasis on law enforcement, I had trainees work a variety of jobs when they were assigned to me. Along with law enforcement, I took them on horseback patrols, helicopter elk counts, packing fish, giving speeches, and whatever presented itself as an opportunity to expand their field experience.

The Department had annual inservice training sessions in all phases of law enforcement for veteran officers. The big difference in wildlife law enforcement and general police work is that wildlife officers more often work alone in back country, whether out on the prairie or high in the mountains. Two-way radio communication into the 1980s was nonexistent in many mountainous areas. Standard operating procedures for police officers did not always apply. We had to be self-reliant.

Carrying a side arm was optional and only a few officers carried one all the time. I carried one once in a while. The culture of being unarmed changed in 1981 when Claude Dallas, an outlaw trapper, murdered two Idaho Conservation Officers. The Division intensified officer survival and self-defense training. Because the state didn't furnish sidearms, we bought our own guns of various calibers and styles. The Division furnished ammunition and required biannual qualification.

The Division provided additional training for arrest techniques and the levels of force that followed law and policy. Officers practiced *Verbal Judo* as a method to defuse highly charged emotional situations to prevent them from becoming physical threats that required a higher level of force. In the early 1990s the Division issued .40 caliber semiautomatic handguns. The training included "shoot-don't shoot" scenarios, use of force, weapon retention, handcuffing techniques and use of batons. Some officers carried MACE and later pepper spray. Before long, my gun belt was loaded down with a sidearm, two extra magazines, baton, handcuffs, packset, and a flashlight. I even carried extra plastic handcuffs in my hatband. How times have changed since the "good-old-days". Over my years of service I was never assaulted although I'd been threatened. Other officers had been assaulted and shot at, but I'm not aware that any of us ever fired our guns at anyone, and I've never heard of a wildlife officer being accused of police brutality or use of excessive force.

Although officer survival training focused on surviving assaults and shootings; nationwide more wildlife officers are killed in the line of duty in vehicle, airplane, and helicopter crashes, drowning and other accidents. John W. Wangnild, DWM in Meeker was killed in a horse accident when he was off duty in June, 2013. Since the 1970s only five Division employees have been killed on the job in Colorado. Four were in plane crashes and Phil Mason's accident.

The Minutemen

The Cold War with the Soviet Union was in the news throughout the 1960s, but wilderness has a way of changing focus from what is going on in the world to what is on the trail in front of you. I was unaware of any danger to me from any outside source. It was the summer of 1968 when I made a three day horseback patrol by myself around the Ute Creek Basin. I contacted fishermen at the six Ute Lakes, plus Rock and Flint Lakes across the Divide. I visited with a number of backpackers. Everyone was pleasant. It was an enjoyable patrol.

When I got home Jim Dyer, an FBI agent, was sitting in our living room. I'd met him before at a Valley Peace Officers meeting. Dyer told me, "We want you to stay out of the Ute Lake country." I told him that I had just spent three days riding that area. He said that he was glad I was home alive. The FBI was trying to catch two federal fugitives. He said that if I would have contacted them, they probably would have killed me. They were heavily armed, possibly with an automatic weapon, and were very dangerous. That really put a scare into me.

Dyer said one of the men [Robert DePugh] was the founder of the Minutemen, an anti-communist terrorist organization in the 1960s. The Minutemen believed communists were going to take over America and they were going to counter attack. The guerrilla group stockpiled weapons, explosives, machine guns, grenades, and other armaments around the country. They threatened and clashed with law enforcement authorities and private citizens whom they thought were a threat to their movement. They had been in the news, but that seemed so far away from Creede.

The FBI had arrested DePugh and others earlier that year for conspiracy to rob a bank and also charged him for violation of federal firearms laws. He was indicted by a federal grand jury in Seattle, Washington. DePugh skipped bail and went underground with an associate. They were survivalists. The FBI had somehow tracked them into the Ute Creek country in the San Juans. That country is so rugged and isolated that the FBI was going to let the snow drive them out of the high country rather than try to find them and risk someone getting hurt or killed. He asked me to keep mum about the threat and felt that they wouldn't bother civilians. As predicted, they left the San Juans and headed south where federal agents arrested them in Truth or Consequences, New Mexico in 1969. After DePugh's arrest, conviction, and imprisonment the Minutemen movement slipped into oblivion. I kept my guard up knowing that my guardian angel was busier than I ever knew.

It looked like murder to me

One summer day in 1985 I was checking fishermen near the Brown Lakes State Wildlife Area when a call came over the radio that there had been a rollover accident, with injuries, only a short distance from me. An ambulance was being dispatched. I radioed that I would meet them at the scene. When I arrived a few people were standing around the upside down SUV. No one appeared hurt and I asked who was injured. No one said anything, but someone pointed above the road. I thought it strange that anyone who was injured would have hiked a few yards and out of sight.

I hiked up the hill with my EMT pack and found a teen-aged boy and girl lying on their backs on the ground. I checked for vital signs, but they were obviously dead. Both of them had been shot in the chest. It looked like murder to me I got down to my truck, and radioed for Burton Smith, the Hinsdale County Sheriff, to come and take over the investigation.

There was one young man wearing a Mexican sarape standing in the crowd that in my mind just didn't fit. I watched him closely until the sheriff arrived and then I left the scene along with the rest of the folks. The young man was arrested and   charged with second degree murder and robbery. He was convicted and sentenced as a juvenile to serve two years and released upon his eighteenth birthday. The three youths were runaways from Illinois.

Kidnap and murder

Bad things seldom happen in little mountain towns. Mineral County Sheriff Phil Leggitt called me to come to his office one morning in June; 1986.I drove into town and found other lawmen who I didn't know huddled in the office. Phil had called in the FBI to handle the kidnapping of a local man.

An FBI agent introduced himself and told me that there was a demand for a ransom. Phil had told him that I was used to flying and knew the Valley. The agent asked me to fly with their pilot and another agent standing by at the airport in case the suspect gave instructions to deliver the ransom money. We could track a vehicle and the money wherever they went.

We waited for several hours until the suspect called. He was kept on the telephone long enough so that agents could trace the call. FBI agents arrested him in a phone booth in Austin, Texas.   In a drug deal gone sour, he confessed to the kidnapping and murder. He gave directions to find the body some eleven miles southeast of Creede. He was extradited back to Colorado where he w a s convicted for the murder and sentenced to life in prison.

The New Jerusalem

It was the day before elk season when I got a call that a man was being brought out of East Willow Creek with a knife wound. The ambulance had been dispatched. I met a pickup truck coming down the jeep road. Men were holding a man prone with a knife stuck in his back. His hunting partners had wisely and skillfully stabilized the knife.

Sheriff Leggitt arrived and we got the story: The hunting party was setting up camp in Phoenix Park when one of the men started acting strangely. He told the men to get on their knees and pray and this being out of character for him, they humored him. He declared that the camp was "The New Jerusalem" [Revelation 21:2,   The Bible] One man began pitching a tent and the suspect came up behind him and shouted that he was Satan and must die and plunged his hunting knife into the victim's back. The rest of the hunting party pulled him away. They administered first aid, loaded the victim into a pickup, and left the assailant alone at camp next to an old miner's shack. We got the victim down to the ambulance.

Phil and I talked it over and since it was getting late we sneaked up to where we could see the cabin, but decided not to approach in the dark. I watched the cabin with my spotting scope and I saw the suspect in the doorway. We knew where he would be in the morning. I called Gordon Saville for help. The next morning Phil sneaked up one side of the creek and I on the other side with guns ready.

We didn't know if there would be a fight, but we had the element of surprise. Gordon was high in the sky in his Cessna. Phil sneaked through the timber to the corner of the cabin. I covered Phil with my rifle. When Phil was ready I gave Gordon the call. He flew down the canyon and just as he swooped low over the cabin, he turned on his siren. The roar of the plane and the sound of a siren caused the suspect to run out to see what the commotion was all about. He was unarmed and surrendered without resistance. Phil handcuffed him and took him into custody. We walked him out to our vehicles and Phil took the suspect to jail in Del Norte. The victim survived the stabbing. The suspect was charged with assault with a deadly weapon, but his defense attorney claimed the defendant was under the influence of cough medicine that caused him to hallucinate. At the state hospital in Pueblo the suspect was declared unfit to stand trial and was sentenced to a mental institution.

"All available lawmen please respond"

Over the years I heard the call for help several times. That was the call that went out across the Valley during an antelope season. Lawmen from all over the Valley responded. I drove toward Saguache. An aerial patrol had spotted the suspect who was a parole violator and was considered armed and dangerous. Sheriff Larry Zimmer sent me with a deputy across a hayfield about five miles south of Saguache to watch for the suspect.

The deputy and I spotted him running towards us. We had been informed that he was an excellent pistol shot and he was pointing it in our direction. I pulled my 30-06 off the rack and chambered a round with the safety on. When he came within twenty-five yards, I told him to stop, drop his gun, and raise his hands. Instead, he stopped, pointed the pistol in his ear and yelled that he would shoot himself (like one of the scenes from the movie *Blazing Saddles*). The deputy yelled, "Go ahead and shoot!"

I told him to give himself up, that nothing was worth dying for, and to walk over to State Highway 285 where Larry and other lawmen waited. They had blocked all the traffic. The suspect walked toward the highway. I lay prone with a solid rest for my rifle and with him in my cross-hairs, but with my trigger finger outside of the trigger guard. I could hear Larry talk to the suspect who was still holding the gun in his ear. Finally, he lowered the gun and gave it to the sheriff. The man could have shot Larry before anyone could have reacted. I wasn't the only one that had him in his sights. Larry's bravery and skill prevailed. He took the suspect into custody.

The Raiders

I never knew what a day would bring. One morning in the summer of 1975 I got a phone call from Bob Hite that an elk was stranded in some rocks in the Rio Grande River. I didn't know Mr. Hite, but drove out to his summer cabin to investigate. Several fishermen were standing outside his cabin. They pointed to what they thought was an elk standing in the river. It did look like an animal, but through my binoculars I could make out that some debris had jammed in some boulders and indeed looked like an animal.

Mr. Hite needlessly apologized and began introducing me to his friends. "Glen, meet General Jimmy Doolittle." We shook hands. I felt like saluting. There I was standing on the banks of the Rio Grande with one of our great American heroes, a Congressional Medal of Honor recipient from World War II.

Mr. Hite hosted an annual gathering of a few of Doolittle's Raiders to fly fish the Rio Grande. I was just a baby when World War II started, but I knew from history that these men were real life American heroes of Tom Brokaw's *Greatest Generation*.

For those young enough to not know of General Doolittle and his "Raiders", he was a pioneer aviator and Colonel in the Army Air Force. He led a flight of sixteen B-25 bombers with eighty crewmen off the aircraft carrier USS Hornet to bomb Japan only four months after the Japanese had bombed Pearl Harbor on December 7, 1941.

They were known as the *Doolittle Raiders*. Bob Hite was the copilot of the last B-25 to take off. After a successful surprise attack the squadron except for one plane flew on to China where they ran out of fuel and crashed. Most of the crews parachuted in the darkness and escaped capture. The attack was more of a psychological victory as it was the first successful attack against Japan since Pearl Harbor. The Japanese captured Mr. Hite and seven other airmen. Three were executed and one died of malnutrition. After being tortured and held in prisons for three and a half years, only four came home.

Doolittle and the other airmen escaped through China and returned to the United States. Colonel Doolittle thought he would be court-martialed for the loss of all the B-25s, but instead was awarded the Congressional Medal of Honor and promoted to General of the Eighth Air Force in the war with Germany. All of the Raiders were awarded the Congressional Gold Medal in May of 2014.

I was honored when Mr. Hite invited me to join the General, his wife Josephine, and other Raiders for lunch. The General raised his glass and toasted to my health. During our table conversation the General explained, "There were thousands of men who did braver things than us [in the war]. We just happened to be there when history came by."

In his autobiography, *I Could Never Be So Lucky Again* [in dedication to his wife] the General wrote of his love to fly fish on the Rio Grande. Later in the day my family had the privilege of meeting the General. He autographed his biography in our World Book Encyclopedia and our son Ralph gave him a dozen of his hand-tied flies. Meeting the Doolittle Raiders was truly one of the most humbling experiences in my life. Even though the General wasn't fishing, he showed me his fishing license and I recorded it in my contact book.

.

Sunrise in the San Juans through The Window after the first snow, Weminuche Wilderness

"Can you hear me now?" Glen calling on a packset from The Window on a summer patrol with Pet (answer was "No.")

CHAPTER 15
Mountains don't care

Mountains don't care if you live or die. I guess that is true for swamps, deserts, jungles, polar ice, oceans, and all other realms of nature. Some people who venture into the wilds get lost. There are numerous Lost Lakes, Lost Creeks, and Lost Trails throughout the Rockies. How did they get lost? Although I've never considered myself as being lost in the mountains, there have been a few times when it took me awhile to get to where I thought I was.

County sheriffs are responsible for search and rescue missions in Colorado. Before the age of organized Search and Rescue (SAR) organizations, county sheriffs knew who to call for help. An ill equipped and untrained volunteer can become a searchee rather than a searcher. Sheriffs in mountainous counties often called the local forest ranger and wildlife officer to assist, because we were the only ones who had two-way radios and communication is a critical component of search and rescue missions. Local volunteers, guides, and other good Samaritans dropped what they were doing to search and rescue the lost and injured.

Dr. Stanley I presume?

Herb Browning, the wildlife officer in Pagosa Springs, called me one morning and asked for help to find a hunter who had been lost for two days on the East Fork of the Piedra River. The closest access was from The Rio Grande side of the Divide. Herb had already called for the regional plane to do an aerial search.

I called Gene Riggs. He got his horse and we rode ten miles to the hunting camp. The outfitter filled us in and that afternoon we made a big circle around the area calling out to the man. We didn't hear or find any sign of him. We rode to a high point where I could call out on a packset. Our plane had not located the missing hunter that day, so I requested that the plane rejoin the search the next morning. I also requested a search team be dispatched. Gene and I spent the night in camp.

Early the next morning we had just saddled our horses when Gordon Saville flew over the area. I told him where we needed him to search and within a few minutes he radioed, "I found him and he's okay." There was a huge sigh of relief throughout the camp. Fortunately the hunter was wearing blaze orange. Using the plane's public address system, Gordon directed him to an opening and a big boulder next to the river where we could get to him on horseback. Gordon then directed us down the East Fork of the Piedra River until we came into an opening and there he was sitting on a big rock looking up at the plane.

I asked, "Dr. Stanley I presume?" Boy was he glad to see us. He had taken good care of himself, but had wandered for three days and was only three miles from camp, but that is a long way in such rugged mountains. We gave him some hot coffee and a snack. We got him back to camp to rejoin his wife and hunting party. With great relief and satisfaction, Gene and I said goodbye and rode back toward our trucks. In the meantime Gordon had flown down Red Mountain Creek and broadcasted to the search party that the hunter was found and to turn around.

Toward the end of his career and with thousands of hours of mountain flying, Gordon was honored to be inducted into the Colorado Aviation Hall of Fame as a result of missions like this. With his flying skills and eagle eyes, he saved a lot of lives, delivered hundreds of emergency messages, found bodies and assisted law enforcement, and the State of Colorado. A friend in the sky-indeed.

The 25 cent search

Phil Leggitt, Mineral County Sheriff, asked for help to search for a an archery hunter who didn't return to an outfitter's camp on at the headwaters of the West Fork of the San Juan River near the Divide Trail in the Weminuche Wilderness. Dave Kenvin and I rode horse back to the isolated camp to assist in the search and provide radio communications with the command post that was set up near Pagosa Springs.

An Army Chinook helicopter from Fort Carson transported search teams and supplies to the camp. The hunter was diabetic and had left camp without taking his insulin. A private helicopter joined the search. In spite of an intensive ground and air search we couldn't find him. Because he was diabetic, the search became a recovery mission when there was no more hope of finding him alive. Phil was flying as an observer when the chopper pilot told him, "I spotted something that doesn't belong." They flew back and located the body. The search was over and Phil notified the family of their loss.

Mineral County was billed $52,000 for the search. Phil said, "That was my total budget for the year." No county sheriff's budget is large enough to handle such unexpected expenses.   In this case the family paid for the private helicopter and other search expenses.

As a result of this search however, Louis Entz the Colorado State Representative from the Valley, drafted legislation to create the Colorado Search and Rescue Fund administered by the Division of Wildlife. Sheriff Leggitt and County Commissioner John Penzien testified in favor of the legislation. There was no opposition.

Initially, the statute added a twenty-five cent surcharge to hunting and fishing licenses and would only reimburse counties for searches for people who had purchased those licenses. Later the surcharge was added to boat, ATV, and snowmobile registration fees and a Colorado Outdoor SAR Card for other outdoors people. All funds were earmarked to reimburse counties for search and rescue missions for license holders and COSAR card holders. Those people who haven't paid into the fund can be held liable for their own search and rescue. The statute was passed in 1987 and in 1996 the Department of Local Affairs began administering the fund.

The fund has reimbursed counties for over 1.5 million dollars for hundreds of SAR missions that were conducted under the authority of county sheriffs. In addition, over six million dollars has been disbursed to county SAR organizations so that volunteers have access to the latest equipment and training available in the country.

EMERGENCY!

Early one spring morning in 1969 I heard a car roaring down the highway. I looked out the window and saw it flip through the air. I assumed someone had to have been hurt. I drove to the scene and found two injured young men lying on the highway. Rod Wintz ran across the road from the Wason Ranch house with blankets. I got my first aid kit out of my truck. County nurse Dorothy Steele and her husband Charles soon arrived in their station wagon that served as Creede's ambulance. Dorothy took charge, administered first aid, and rushed them to the Del Norte hospital where they were treated. Both survived the crash, but their prom suits didn't fare so well.

Later, I talked to Dorothy about my frustration that I had been at the scene of several traffic accidents and didn't know what to do and my state first aid kit only had some band aids and supplies for a minor. Dorothy told me about a new program that was just getting started in Colorado.

Only five volunteers from each county in the Valley could participate in a 120 hour training program to become Emergency Medical Technicians (EMTs). I found that being an EMT was one of the ways I could contribute to the community.

Sheriff Harry Larson, rancher Charles Steele, city marshal Richard Fairchild, and REA lineman Frank Foote and I volunteered to take the course. We drove fifty-two miles every week all winter long to Monte Vista and were certified as the first EMTs in Mineral County. We used the sheriff's car for our first "ambulance" run.

We didn't have an ambulance, but before long Creede had some bake sales and enough donations to buy a used ambulance that had state of the art equipment, but didn't have a two-way radio. When we got a call, the sheriff, city marshal or I radioed the State Patrol dispatcher to notify the Del Norte hospital that our ambulance was enroute. The 911 emergency phone service was not available in rural areas. Instead, our five phone numbers were listed on a sticky label that people pasted onto their telephones. It wasn't long until we had a two-way radio in the ambulance and a county dispatch center to handle emergency calls. I was on call 24/7 both for the D i v i s i o n and for ambulance service

In 1971 twenty-seven new Creede EMTs were certified to serve a community that had grown to nearly 1,000 residents because of a resurgence of silver mining. The experiences I had while serving twenty years as an EMT were some of most rewarding of my career. I had the privilege of being a charter member of the Colorado EMT Association and chairman of the San Luis Valley Emergency Medical Services (EMS) Council.

Prior to 1972 an ambulance attendant was not required to have even Standard Red Cross First Aid training. Harry Larson and I testified before a State House of Representative committee on EMS. They were debating whether to pass a law requiring ambulance services to have certified EMTs as attendants. A few small communities objected on the basis that getting the training and equipment was too much of a hardship. Harry and I testified that if little old Creede could provide high level EMS then any community could do the same. Representatives from the Colorado Department of Emergency Services and the Colorado EMT Association pledged to provide the training and help to purchase state of the art equipment. The bill passed.

When the EMT program was in its early development there were no protocols between EMTs, hospitals, law enforcement, and doctors. The 1972 television show "Emergency!" was the first exposure the public had about professional emergency medical care. The public was also becoming aware of military paramedics performing heroic lifesaving missions in Vietnam. The San Luis Valley EMS Council was created to establish protocols. Doctors and other medical professionals developed the high level of instruction to what it is today. We soon had two-way adio communications between EMTs and hospitals so that doctors could direct the care of patients. What we did in the Valley was being accomplished statewide. The accomplishments of America's local EMS systems and the thousands of EMTs and paramedics are legendary. We owe them our gratitude and in some cases, our lives.

High angle rescue

Even though EMTs were proving their value to our community two events in one summer demonstrated that we needed more specialized training

Alan Czencush belays EMT during training exercise for high angle rescue

The last call for search and rescue for an overdue hiker was on Red Mountain, south of Creede. I called Gordon Saville. In the meantime a rescue team from South Fork led by Ernie Wilkinson responded. I must add here that Ernie Wilkinson was ahead of his time in teaching survival skills and was the leader of a well trained and equipped SAR team in the Valley.

Gordon and I began flying contours around the mountain and he shouted, "There he is!" I didn't see what he was looking at so Gordon circled back and dipped his wing to point to the young man's body at the top of a dry waterfall. He had fallen off a cliff. Gordon made another pass, flying so close to the mountain that I could see that he was dead.

Gordon dropped me off at the airport

High angle rescue training with Ralph Hinshaw as our "patient" circa 1974

Hiker had fallen from a cliff down to the brink of a dry waterfall. Adams State College Rescue Team belays Glen and the body down to Larry Ehardt and Gene Dooley Photos by Ernest Wilkinson

and I joined the search, which we knew was a recovery. The recovery team climbed up a rock slide and when we got to the bottom of the waterfall, we had no way to climb the near vertical face, let alone get the body down. I radioed to Gordon who was circling above and he relayed a message to the Alamosa dispatcher to request the Adams State College Mountain Rescue Team again. Gordon flew to Alamosa and picked up two climbers and their gear.

They joined us and climbed to the top of the waterfall. The coroner asked me as an EMT to verify the death. So, I had my first climbing lesson on the spot. After this experience we contacted Alan Czencush who was working for the San Luis Valley Emergency Medical Services (EMS) Council. Alan had been a member of the Western State College's [University] mountain rescue team. He set up training sessions for those EMTs who were able and willing to learn how to safely conduct high angle rescues. We equipped our ambulance with all the climbing gear that we needed to safely rescue people in dangerous situations. Creede is but one example of how mountain communities respond to the kinds of dangers unique to their environment. Likewise, prairie and metropolitan EMTs are equipped and trained to handle emergencies in those areas. We are in good hands.

Back country friends-indeed

The Division had been training new officers in Standard Red Cross First Aid for many years. In the 1970s many new officers had been in the military and already had more advanced training than the Standard Red Cross course. All trainees had a minimum of a Bachelor of Science degree and wanted

Mike Zgainer and Glenn Eyre and other officers carry a "patient" on an improvised stretcher during a training exercise

more substance in this aspect of their training. I met with Clyde Slonaker, Division Training Officer, and told him about my experience of being inadequately trained and equipped and that I had completed EMT training and assembled my own EMT kit. Because we were public servants, I suggested that the Division upgrade the level of medical emergency training. He asked me to come up with a plan. I contacted the chief of Colorado EMS, who gave me a copy of the EMT lesson plans.

Officers Steve Bissell, Glenn Smith, and I adapted a curriculum for the trainee program which we called Medical Emergency Training (MET) at the next training session. The course was well received and we arranged for EMT instructors in the regions to teach the course. Slonaker saw the value of the training and hired paramedics to teach the MET course, which is similar to the current first responder training.

Alan Czencush, who had come to work for the Division as a temporary employee at the time, and I developed a scenario-based MET training program. We patterned the training similar to that of EMT practical exercises to teach patient evaluation, the basis for proper care of the sick or injured. In this refresher course we coached 'victims' and used realistic appearing wounds to garner appropriate responses. Officers improvised treatment from whatever was on hand in their trucks to perform back country rescue and care. This training was done in each region of the state. Some officers soon found themselves in situations where they implemented the skills that they learned.

The lack of an adequate first aid kit was evident. Alan developed a supply list and the Division assembled and distributed MET kits to field personnel. On their own initiative some Division personnel became EMTs, serving in their local communities. If you're hurt in the back country, a wildlife officer can be your best friend-indeed.

Whirly birds to the rescue

In the 1970s commercial helicopter rescue services were not available in most rural areas of Colorado. The Fort Carson Army Base near Colorado Springs had a MAST (Military Assistance to Safety and Traffic) unit for civilian rescue missions. Most of these pilots and crews were Vietnam veterans. The Army flew a MAST helicopter from the 8th Medical Detachment to Creede in the summer of 1972 to train EMTs in safety procedures when working around a helicopter. That big Huey got a lot of attention as it landed right in front of the Mineral County Medical Center. EMTs spent part of the day in training with the Army crew. This opportunity was also good PR for the Army.

Three days later I got a phone call for help about 4:00 o'clock in the morning. Bev and Mike McClure and Kim Wintz had backpacked to Vallecito Lake, a small alpine lake nestled at 12,000 feet above sea level in a cirque basin at the headwaters of Vallecito Creek. Bev was unpacking when a single action .22 caliber revolver fell out of a duffle bag and discharged, hitting her in the chest. Mike gave her first aid. He hiked over the Divide after midnight to Beartown [a ghost town] where another Creede resident, Jim Cook was camped. Mike returned to his wife while Jim drove to the nearest telephone at Rio Grande Reservoir and called me.

I called Fort Carson and talked to the soldier in charge. He called back in a few minutes and said they were on their way and would meet me at the Creede airport. Soon after sunrise I heard that distinctive Huey droning "whump-whump". It is difficult to describe, but once you hear a Huey's distinctive sound it is burned into your mind forever. I identified myself and the commander asked me if I could guide them to the lake. We circled and the pilot selected a landing zone. I was looking out the nose of the chopper and it looked to me like we were flying into a rock wall, but the pilot skillfully landed on the ledge next to their camp. The medic and a medical doctor went to Bev's side and ministered to her wound. The bullet hadn't penetrated her chest as was feared. The doctor administered pain medication and we loaded her into the chopper.

The pilot began liftoff, but then settled back to the ground several times. I didn't know it at the time, but he was burning off excess fuel to lighten the load. There were seven of us onboard, including the pilot, commander (also a pilot), crew chief, medic, doctor, Bev, and me. Finally, we lifted off, cleared the ledge, turned and it felt to me like we were dropping like a rock into the Vallecito Creek canyon below. We picked up some forward airspeed and began a slow climb out of the canyon, back over the Divide, and set a course to the Monte Vista Hospital.

We landed at the helipad in Monte Vista and carried Bev into the hospital. Afterwards as I was giving my headset to the pilot I complimented him for what I thought was some pretty tough flying. He asked, "Were you scared?" I told him no, that I was used to counting elk from a chopper. I asked, "Should I have been?" He answered, "Sir, I have been shot at and shot down in Vietnam and I have never been as scared as when we lifted off that ledge." Shivers went up my spine when he said that one of the cardinal rules of flying choppers was to never pull full power and "At 12,000 feet we nearly pulled the guts out of that ship getting out of there." I told him that he and his crew were the coolest and calmest men I had ever been around. I couldn't tell from their intercom conversations that this mission was anything out of the ordinary for them. I learned the meaning of the cliché "ignorance is bliss." Bev was treated and released.

Another time I was on patrol when I my citizens band radio crackled "Breaker one nine for The Brushfuzz", my CB handle. Jack Jordan MD was calling for help. We met and he explained that he was on his way to Ernie Wilkinson's archery hunting camp near the Rio Grande Pyramid. Ernie's son Larry met Dr. Jordan on the trail and told him that his brother Jerold was sick with appendicitis.

Trusting in Ernie's diagnosis, Dr. Jordan turned around, came down to a phone and requested a MAST rescue mission. He showed me where the camp was on a map and asked if I could guide the chopper to the camp while he went to the Monte Vista Hospital to prepare the emergency room.

In a couple hours the chopper picked me up at the Creede airport and we flew to the area. I knew Ernie would have a signal and landing zone. Sure enough, we spotted him in a small clearing waving his shiny space blanket. The pilot skillfully maneuvered between the towering spruce trees and landed right next to Jerold.

The medic made his examination and we loaded Jerold into the chopper and headed out as the sun was going down. After dropping me off in Creede they flew on to Monte Vista. Dr. Jordan called me later to say that had we not brought Jerold out when we did that he may not have survived. His appendix had ruptured.

As in Bev McClure's rescue, my role was miniscule. I was humbled and thankful to be a tiny part of these missions of mercy. Today, commercial helicopter services provide back-country air rescues with the same high level of professionalism and c r e w s risking their lives to serve the public.

We spotted Ernie's camp next to a
tiny island of tall spruce trees

Looking over the pilots shoulder at
Ernie with his space blanket signal

Ernie and the pilot watch as the Army medic examines Jerold

MAST chopper flying Jerold to the Monte Vista Hospital for emergency surgery
Photo by Ernest Wilkinson

Avalanche

Avalanches have been one of the leading causes of winter deaths in the San Juan Mountains since the late 1800s when the first prospectors and miners came in search of wealth. More recently back country travelers, snowmobilers, and skiers have fallen victim to avalanches.

Darrell McKee was one of my Boy Scouts. He went snowshoeing alone above Creede in Windy Gulch when he was buried in an avalanche. Darrell's older brother Jack shares their story:

> "Darrell was about 14 years old and I was 16. He had taken off on his snowshoes. He had been gone longer than we thought, but I was not worried. Mom got more and more worried as it got later and later. Finally, she convinced me to go look for him. I was wading in waist deep snow climbing up Windy Gulch when I could faintly hear him. I found a deep pile of snow with a fist-sized hole in it and a very frightened voice coming out of it. The whole hillside of snow had come down on him, but he managed to get his hand loose and make a hole so he could breathe. I dug down through the hard packed snow to a snowshoe, removed it, and used it to dig him out. Then I put the snowshoes on and carried him on my back to the road. It was about dark when Charles and Dorothy Steele met me and took him to the hospital to be treated for hypothermia. Fortunately, he didn't suffer any frostbite. He came through the ordeal without any physical problems."

Although I was not involved in any way with this incident, I was profoundly impacted by the near loss of one of my Boy Scouts and later it influenced me to take avalanche training.

Two men were hunting elk on the west side of Pole Mountain, near the headwaters of the Rio Grande River in 1971. An early season snowstorm had dumped three feet of snow in the San Juans. As the two stalked just below timberline they walked into an avalanche chute. They heard a loud "crack" above them and the white death swept one hunter away. The other hunter's rifle sling snagged on a little tree and he held on for dear life and survived.

Virgil Mason, the sheriff of San Juan County in Silverton got word of the tragedy and called me to help. Snow drifts had closed access over the Continental Divide at Stony Pass. I requested an experienced mountain rescue team from Adams State College join the search. I relayed Greg Simmons and his team to the hunting camp at the confluence of the Rio Grande and Pole Creek by snowmobile. The sheriff and some rescuers from Silverton flew in by helicopter. I found a place above Rio Grande Reservoir where I had radio contact with the State Patrol dispatcher in A l a m o s a. When Virgil needed to communicate, he called me on his packset and I relayed his message to Silverton via dispatchers in Alamosa and Durango and vice-versa.

Recovery efforts were suspended for six days when avalanche conditions became more extreme. Virgil radioed to me that the camp was running out of food. I bought some groceries and asked Gordon Saville to make an aerial food drop. Gordon swooped down Pole Creek and I pushed the rations out the door into the snow next to their camp. While we were in the area we flew the high country looking for stranded hunting camps, but all of them were able to get to lower country.

Virgil and his crew stayed on the mountain. One of the Denver newspapers had written a story that was a little short on the facts. Because of that article, worried wives kept called our house and inundated Virgil's office with calls. When there was absolutely no hope of Survival. I suggested that we notify the

A handler directs an avalanche search dog to find a buried "victim" near Molas Pass. Circa 1973

family to ease the public concern. Since Virgil was out of touch with his office he asked me to notify the family and release the victim's name to the press.

The body was found on the sixth day at the bottom of a cliff buried under six feet of snow. He had suffered a broken neck and had died instantly. During that same storm wildlife officer Dick Weldon was busy helping the Army evacuate some high country hunting camps in the South San Juan Wilderness. The snow was up to five feet deep with even deeper drifts. Wranglers had to b r e a k trail for their horses to get to lower country. After that experience avalanche danger was on my mind every time it snowed.

In 1973 Virgil Mason and Don Fritch ree stablished the San Juan Avalanche Project that had been started in 1962 to teach avalanche safety to Forest Service personnel and ski patrolmen. With more cross country skiers and snowmobilers going into the back country and the inherent danger to them and rescuers, they expanded the training to include first responders. Virgil invited me to attend. Having nearly lost one of my boy scouts to an avalanche and being in a support role in the Pole Mountain avalanche, I was anxious to get some avalanche training. As with so many other search and rescue missions, I called upon Gene Riggs to go with me for the training. We met some of the men who worked on the Pole Mountain avalanche recovery team.

The workshop covered all aspects of avalanches including snow metamorphous, dynamics of avalanches, survival, planning rescues and recovery, and conducting searches with avalanche dogs, probe lines and the newly developed avalanche beacon. After attending that avalanche school I became more aware of my surroundings when I was in the back country during the winter months. Gene utilized the training when he guided snowmobile trips and taught snowmobile safety classes. I still don't buy white sheets.

Lightning

Of all the dangers I faced, one element of nature was always on my mind when I rode the high country. John Stewart and I had just changed the water chart on the Piedra Diversion and were riding across a rock slide near the top of South River Peak. It was late afternoon and that was no place to be near 13,000 feet when lightning started flashing. We were far above timberline and there was no place to hide. We dismounted, separated from each other and our horses, and squatted down to reduce the chance of being struck. By separating ourselves we reduced the chance of a strike killing both of u s . As with most passing storms, the threat soon ended and we rode down to Goose Lake to check fishermen and camp for the night. It was another electrifying experience.

John Stewart dismounts and prepares to wait out the lightning on South River Peak   circa 1970

In 1976 a pack train including nine horsemen were riding the Continental Divide trail only a short distance from where John Stewart and I had our encounter with lightning on South River Peak, when lightning from an approaching thunderstorm struck. One man was killed instantly and three were injured. Everyone was thrown from their horses. Nine horses were killed and the remainder stampeded off the mountain. Herb Browning, the wildlife officer from Pagosa Springs, was in the lead.

The survivors attended to the injured. They hiked about a mile off the mountain and found refuge in the Division's Piedra cabin. They were wet and cold, but were able to start a fire and eat food that was in the cabin. The next morning Herb hiked nine miles to the Ivy Creek Campground and had to commandeer a car when the driver refused to take him to a phone, because "I don't want to get involved." A search party from Creede responded to retrieve the body and what gear was on the ground. I was working on a project in the Valley when I got the call from Herb, but by the time I got half way to the cabin, the search party was bringing everyone out.

We took everyone to the Creede Hotel and even though the dining room was closed, the proprietor cranked up the grill and fed the survivors and search party. When Herb asked to pay the bill, the proprietor said he wouldn't accept a check or money, because he couldn't go on the search, and it was his way of helping and expressing his sympathy. I was so proud of our community.

The survivors bedded down for the night at our house and the bunkhouse next door. The next day we relayed them back to Pagosa Springs. A few days after that some of the party rode back to find the horses that had survived.

Lightning struck again near the Freemon Ranch. EMTs responded to a call for a wrangler who had been struck by lightning near the Freemon Ranch. When we arrived we found the young man conscious but incoherent. His vitals were strong. We rushed him to the Del Norte Hospital where he was stabilized and we learned later he had survived.

Several years later I was walking out of church and overheard a young man talking about being struck by lightning. I asked him if he was the wrangler that we had attended to and he said yes. He didn't remember any of the incident, so I told him what we as EMTs did. Then he explained what the lightning did to him. It blew a hole in his hat, ruptured his ear drums, burned the bottom of his feet where the nails were in his boots, welded two quarters to his car keys in his pocket, blew a hole in the saddle and killed his horse. It was a miracle he survived. Surgeons repaired his ear drums. He was married with a couple children and living "close to God."

Lightning killed livestock as well. I investigated the deaths of nine cows on Grassy Hill below Stony Pass. A bear had scavenged some of the carcasses. It was apparent that the cows had gathered close together during a thunderstorm when lightning struck and killed all nine of them. The carcasses were all scorched.

The Rio Grande Pyramid and the "Window" as viewed from Glenn Lake (one of the Ute Lakes). Weminuche Wilderness

CHAPTER 16
The fork in the trail

"When you come to a fork in the road, take it." Yogi Berra

When you reach the top of a mountain a whole new horizon presents itself. I had reached my goal and lived the dream of being a Wildlife Officer in the mountains. We had been in the Creede District for twenty-one years and I was beginning to have symptoms of burnout. I had worked hard to perpetuate the wild places and wildlife of the Upper Rio Grande and the San Juan Mountains. I loved the people of Creede, the Valley, and the thousands of visitors that came each year.

Lois and Ralph grew up so fast. Both of them were salutatorians of their graduating classes. Both of them went on to college and graduated. Ralph married Alice Jensen of Norwood. The churches all had pastors and I felt it might be time for me to leave my beloved Creede. I was torn. Every bend in the trail reflected echoes from the past, but the sense of adventure had left me. My enthusiasm for wildlife had not waned, but I was approaching a fork in the trail.

Meg Gallagher, the Southwest Regional Information and Education Specialist, resigned her position in 1987. I applied for the job and even though I didn't have the required degree in journalism, personnel rules allowed for the substitution of experience for the degree. Using my daily diaries, I documented enough experience to be allowed to apply for the job.

I had written a weekly column, press releases, radio programs, slide shows and lectures, along with training and experience for handling controversies. I had taught in classrooms, hunter education, trained Project WILD teachers and facilitators chaired a School Improvement Committee, trained EMTs, and even coached wrestling. I took written and oral exams and got the job.

In the spring of 1988 Beth and I watched a moving van take our belongings to Montrose. My eyes got a little misty as we left Creede. Goal setting is important, but it has been the journey in life; my family, the experiences, the people, the land, and my relationship with God that transcends all my failures and achievements.

What do I do now?

I sat at my desk that first morning in the Montrose office and asked myself that very question. Regional Manager Bob Towry a n d I made a plan. I toured the region to meet the newspaper publishers and radio station managers. It was a real joy to tour the southwest corner of Colorado where I had already worked for twenty-five years. Director Jim Rusch changed the title of my position from Information and Education Specialist to Public Liaison. It was my job to provide wildlife information to reporters who wrote the stories, just like I had done when I started my career in Cortez. I did write some press releases for small t o w n newspapers, but I was out of my league writing for large newspapers. For several weeks, Todd Malmsbury, Information Chief, patiently coached me in the art of writing and editing. The Denver and regional I & E staff bent over backwards to help me succeed.

During my oral interview I was asked, "Do you know how to operate a dark room?" I answered, "Turn off the light." No o n e used a dark room anymore. Digital technology was already changing the communications field. Computers were brand new. I didn't even know how to turn one on. Typing had been one of my strong points since high school and learning word processing skills came easy.

The other major role of the position was wildlife education. Project Wild was developed by thirteen western states to provide teachers with K-12 activities centered on wildlife. I participated in one of the last writing sessions and was on the team who taught the first Project Wild facilitators. Through that outreach program the Division provided wildlife curriculum enhancement activities and materials for teachers. I had the privilege of participating with other education staff to lead teacher workshops as well as training facilitators to teach their own workshops. Through this project the Division enhanced the knowledge of thousands of children about wildlife.

Rough trail ahead

After we had been in Montrose a short time we closed on the purchase of a house. The next day Bob called me into his office and told me that there had been a State Personnel Board action and I was bumped out of my position. I was in limbo for several months wondering what was going to happen to me. Among other assignments, Dave Langlois, the Regional Aquatic Biologist, requested that I put together an in-house reference book, *The Back Country Lakes of Southwest Colorado*. I had the privilege of flying with Jim Olterman to take aerial photographs of back country lakes in the San Juans, Grand Mesa, Gunnison, and the Valley. I merged a physical data base with the pictures. This book gave pilots and biologists accurate information about the location and data about each lake in the region.

Then one morning in 1990, with my family around me I suffered a brain seizure. I recovered and before long I was able to return to work, but not allowed to drive for six months. I hitched rides around the region conducting public meetings, until I got my driving privileges restored.

During this time our marriage began to break up and ended in divorce in 1993. My life was upside down and out of my control. I turned to my faith believing that ". . . all things work together for good." God gave me a special kind of grace and peace that can't be explained. I chose to move ahead. I never lost my enthusiasm for life, wildlife, and people.

The regional demand for information and education had become more than what one person could handle. As Regional Manager, Bob took the initiative to establish a new job. Our new director Perry Olson approved the creation of the position. Geoff Tischbein had been the Southwest Regional I&E Specialist before Meg Gallagher and he returned to Montrose as the Information Specialist and I became the Southwest Regional Education Coordinator. The other regions soon followed suit.

I continued having Project Wild teacher workshops. I expanded the education outreach by coordinating the educational programs of other agencies and organizations throughout the southwest region. Instead of presenting competing and sometimes conflicting programs, we began working together by supporting school districts with more comprehensive opportunities for teachers and students. We could not add to teacher's workloads, but we gave them the resources to help them accomplish their curriculum standards.

The Division had a library of 16mm movies, but schools were changing to VHS videos. I used a portion of my budget to have some of the movies converted to VHS. I developed a regional resource catalogue and several education kits that teachers could check out. It is a never ending challenge to keep up with the changing technology and the opportunities it offers. The other regional education coordinators and Denver staff developed more resources for teachers. About the time I retired, the Internet opened a whole new opportunity to provide information and resources.

Regional coordinators attended national conferences to learn what other states were doing. We brought back some good ideas from other states, but we learned that Colorado was among several nationally recognized states for its wildlife education outreach.

I was a member of the National Association for Environmental Education and went to several of their conferences. I didn't have a formal education background so it was a wonderful opportunity to take in many workshops and seminars to get onto the cutting edge of environmental education and education in general.

I was invited to give a presentation at an international conference in Cancun, Mexico where I shared with educators from far and wide how we brought diverse agencies and organizations together as we had done in the southwest region of Colorado.

The State of Idaho sponsored a Project WILD national conference in McCall, Idaho that got a little on the wild side. It was most memorable for Tom Lines, the Northwest Regional Education Coordinator, and Kirk Madariaga, Wildlife Officer from Paonia and me. We decided to take some free time and go see the famous Salmon River, "The River of No Return" at Riggins, Idaho.

On a short drive down the river below Riggins we saw a blue raft with five people enjoying a float trip. We had driven down river from Riggins to just see that famous river. We turned around and on the way back toward town we saw two people swimming and the raft had flipped. It was May and the water was cold. We knew they weren't swimming for the fun of it. They were wearing life jackets. We turned around and raced to the bridge below town to intercept them. We could hear the woman screaming for help as they floated under the bridge. The husband was swimming a side stroke and pulled his wife into the eddy below the bridge. Kirk and Tom grabbed the wife. I grabbed the husband. He immediately lost consciousness. I held on to him and another man showed up and we pulled him out of the cold water. An ambulance arrived with EMTs and the couple was taken to a hospital. I'm sure the husband ran out of adrenaline, his body exhausted, and hypothermic. He saved both of their lives. We were just there to help at the end of their ordeal. As a result we were late in getting back to the conference.

When we got back, Perry Olson, our Director, asked us where we had been. He noted that we had missed his opening speech and we were AWOL. I explained that God sent us to s a v e some lives and He had seniority.

The following winter we were surprised to see our rescue on the television program *Rescue 911*. The episode was filmed on location, but featured a kayaker saving them, when in reality he didn't show up until after we got them out of the river. The narrative did emphasize correctly that the husband saved his wife.

The Division hosted an "Outdoor Adventure Workshop" near Salida, Colorado for sixty teachers for several summers. Regional education coordinators put together a five day course in which teachers earned college credit. Most of the time was spent outdoors exposing teachers to Project WILD. Dozens of volunteer instructors taught plant, animal and aquatic insect identification, orienteering (before the days of GPS), shooting sports, archery, a float trip down the Arkansas River, fly tying and casting, and how to incorporate new found knowledge into their curriculum. This intense workshop was a life changing experience for some teachers. Budget restrictions put an end to the workshop, because it was so labor intensive and didn't reach enough teachers-a quality vs quantity decision.

One of my most satisfying experiences occurred while I was at an inservice training session in Estes Park, Colorado. I was looking for a cousin's phone number in nearby Allenspark. Just below his name was the name "Richard Inglis". I couldn't resist. I called and asked, "Are you the Mr. Inglis who taught biology at North High School in Denver back in the 1950s?" He answered, "Yes." I told him who I was and he remembered me. He asked me why I called and I told him how I found his name and said, "I wanted to tell you that you were one of the best and most influential teachers I ever had." He thanked me and asked me what I was doing. I told him, "I am influencing teachers to be like you." I can't think of a better compliment to give a teacher and I was fortunate to make contact after all those years and say, "You made a difference. Thank you."

Keeping my finger on the trigger

After moving to Montrose I maintained my law enforcement commission by going to inservice training sessions and qualifying with firearms twice a year. I helped district officers during the hunting seasons and filled in for them throughout the region. I videotaped several searches. Although law enforcement was never my strong suit, it was still in my blood.

The Division provided an unusual training session at Fort Carson. I'd been through a lot of training, but this was pretty heavy stuff. Most of the training was at the felony level. We practiced making felony arrests, searching booby-trapped buildings for armed felons, and other high threat officer survival scenarios. Some Colorado Springs police officers volunteered as "bad guys" who challenged our training and experience. Since wildlife officers so seldom face felony situations I wondered why such intensity?

A couple years later Bob called me into his office and asked me if I could lead a watchable wildlife tour in the Valley on a certain date. I marked my calendar and on the day before, he called me into his office and asked if I was prepared to go and I said that I was. He closed the door and said he would pick me up at four o'clock in the morning and to bring my sidearm, body armor, shotgun, and EMT pack. I asked, "For a watchable wildlife tour?" He answered that he couldn't tell me anymore and instructed me to tell no one of our conversation. That evening he called me at home and said that my services wouldn't be needed after all, but I would find out the next morning what was going on.

The next morning Geoff Tischbein came running out of his office exclaiming, "You aren't going to believe what is going on!" Operation SLV or The Raid as it became known to us, was a culmination of a three year covert operation by the U.S. fish and Wildlife Service in the Valley. The reason for that unusual training we had at Fort Carson became apparent. In some cases officers were dealing with some hard core criminals. My role was to have been an aerial coordinator, because I knew the Valley; however, another officer who knew that area of the Valley even better than I, was given that assignment at the last minute.

A task force of about 275 federal and state wildlife officers made an unprecedented predawn raid in the Valley, northern New Mexico and several other states. The Raid resulted in 103 felony convictions for commercial wildlife trafficking and other wildlife crimes. At that time it was one of the largest wildlife raids in the nation's history. This was a great moment for wildlife justice that so many of us had worked so hard for over the years. (A detailed account of Operation SLV is found in the book *The Thin Green Line* authored by Terry Grosz, USFWS Special Agent, who coordinated The Raid.)

I carried a law enforcement commission for thirty-two years, but the demands of my job prevented me from continuing the required training and time dedicated to law enforcement. The day I handed in my sidearm, ticket book, and other paraphernalia was like giving up part of my soul. I was second only to Palisade District Officer Jim Miller in seniority, but I had lost that fine edge that it takes to survive in our changing culture. I had no regrets.

Public sector problem solving

For decades governmental agencies had the attitude that "The public be damned, we'll do what we want." Political pressure began to change the landscape of public service. Agencies began holding public meetings and field trips; however, that didn't mean they were really listening. Some of these efforts were interpreted as just selling a management project.

When people yell and scream it means they feel nobody is listening. When people raise their voices, brains turn off, and meetings are unproductive. The public needs to understand however, that even though an agency listens, its legislated mission must not be compromised. Only the legislature can change its mandated mission. The purpose of gathering public input should be to develop consensus to solve problems, not sell a particular agenda. Almost any solution creates a problem for someone else and this is a dilemma.

Bob Towry, Harvey Donoho and I took an advanced "Public Sector Problem Solving" course at the Asilomar Conference Center in Monterey, California. That training was soon put to the test. Since the 1930s, game damage to agricultural interests has faced the Division. The issue came to a head in the San Juan Basin in the early 1990s. The Wildlife Commission and director instructed the regions to conduct meetings to gather public input.

Since I was the public liaison I was on the regional team. We developed a plan to objectively listen and report the outcome of a series of meetings. Our first meeting was in Durango. I sent invitations to about forty people who represented a cross section of interested citizens. Just before that meeting a "bombshell" fell out of nowhere.

Someone had written what appeared to be an internal Division memo describing the *"San Juan Project"* a clandestine plan for the Division to use the power of eminent domain (which it never had) to condemn and seize private ranches for big game range in the San Juan Basin. This 'memo' infuriated ranchers and politicians.

The Division had an 'Ace' to play. At the beginning of this process I sent invitations on Division letterhead that I customized. The names of wildlife commissioners were listed at the bottom of the letterhead. I replaced two outgoing commissioners' names with two new names. No other updated letterhead existed. Someone who received my invitation merely blanked out the text and wrote the 'memo', made copies, and mailed them to some key people.

A hostile audience came to cast stones. One man even challenged me to a fight in the parking lot. As people entered the meeting room however, they looked at a display of the fraudulent 'memo'. The high emotional level lowered to a point in which people presented their concerns, complaints, and recommendations. We truly listened. We reported the public's input to the director and Wildlife Commission and defused a volatile situation.

New assignments

The Wildlife Commission directed the Division to create formal volunteer and watchable wildlife programs. Each region decided how to implement these new mandates. The decisions were based on the question, "Whose plate (of the regional staff) is the most empty?" Each region established its own lines of responsibility and budgeting.

Linda Fox was the Division's first state volunteer coordinator and Bob Hernbrode was the first watchable wildlife coordinator. These two leaders worked with the regional staff coordinators to get these programs started. I was assigned to be the southwest regional education, watchable wildlife, and volunteer coordinator. I spent most of my time going to meetings with other coordinators and agencies. I hate meetings, but we got some good programs started.

Colorado hosted the second annual National Watchable Wildlife Conference in 1995 in Estes Park. Representatives from all across the United States came at the height of the elk bugling in Rocky Mountain National Park. Representatives from numerous agencies and organizations put together a showpiece conference.

The Southwest Region had already developed some watchable wildlife opportunities before the reorganization. The Alamosa and Monte Vista National Wildlife Refuges, the Division, and other organizations hosted the Monte Vista Crane Festival which drew thousands of people every spring to see the annual spring migration of Greater Sandhill Cranes and dozens of other species of water birds.

Geoff Tischbein and I had produced a watchable wildlife brochure for the Valley that highlighted viewing opportunities. I worked with district officers and area biologists throughout the region to develop viewing and interpretive sites. To learn more about this phase of my responsibilities I attended a National Park Service interpretive inservice training session. I consulted with State Parks and U.S. Forest Service interpreters to develop watchable wildlife opportunities in Colorado's state parks and scenic byways in the southwest region.

Volunteers have contributed so much to perpetuate wildlife in Colorado. A formal volunteer program increased the number of volunteers who were anxious to work on wildlife projects. Young people who are interested in a wildlife career can find that being a wildlife volunteer is a good way to learn about wildlife management and work alongside of wildlife professionals, just like I did in high school.

We soon had volunteer leaders in each area, who worked hand in hand with wildlife officers and biologists. More than contributing to wildlife, volunteers developed a vested interest in wildlife. The program also provided the Division a more formal way of saying "Thank You" for their contributions to wildlife.

Bob sent me to a Colorado Supervisor Training Course for a new responsibility. In addition to other duties I became the regional office supervisor. Supervising four women was a new challenge that no amount of training could actually prepare me for. I thought I was up to the task when we had our first staff meeting.

The ladies brought me up to date on office issues. I listened intently. At the end of the meeting I asked if there was anything I could do, as their supervisor, to enhance the work place? One of the secretaries, answered, "Hinshaw, you stay out of our way!" I said, "Yes ma'am." I assumed my new role, did as I was told, and I do believe that we had the most professional, efficient, effective, and pleasant office in the State of Colorado.

The Division began a major reorganization in 1994 that in my opinion was really needed. Over time the lines of authority, responsibility, and budgeting were all mixed up. I had responsibilities with no authority to make decisions or a budget to implement programs and projects for which I was only partially responsible. Under the reorganization I was assigned to be the Education

Coordinator for the western slope of Colorado. I no longer had so many responsibilities and new personnel were hired for the watchable wildlife, volunteer programs and supervision of the regional office.

Soon after the reorganization was finished, the State Personnel Board announced in the summer of 1997 that the regional education position would be downgraded and we would have a twenty-percent cut in salary. With thirty-four years of service, it was a no-brainer. I retired in December of 1997. I value the relationships I had with my coworkers and the public that supported the wise use and perpetuation of our natural resources.

I married Carol Kelton, a retired Texas school teacher in 1995 and we wanted to travel. We shared the same faith and our love for the outdoors. We enjoyed rafting several western rivers, hiking in British Columbia, photography, swimming, touring the outer banks of North Carolina and traveled from coast to coast and border to border. I had lived my dreams and I never looked back, but never quit caring about wild places and wildlife.

CHAPTER 17
Writing down the trail

It has been said that the only real constant in this world is change. Writing down this trail has verified the truth of that statement in my life. Whether it is people and their attitudes or the environment, change happens. Some changes are only slight and others have tremendous and wide spread impacts that last for centuries. Such was the case in the San Juan Mountains in the summer of 2013.

Fire on the mountain

The ecology of the land is dynamic. Even mountains move. Some changes take millennia and some just a few days. For centuries there have been small fires in the San Juan Mountains that have created a mosaic of forest and meadow. The forest was nicknamed *The Asbestos Forest*, typical of high altitude spruce forests, because there had been no large fires in several centuries. Engelmann spruce trees mature in 100 years and live up to 400 years. As the forest reaches maturity it is far more susceptible to disease and insects such as the spruce bark beetle. The latter stages of a climax forest are not as productive from a wildlife standpoint.

Since 1996 the spruce bark beetle had infested nearly 500,000 acres of the Rio Grande National Forest and another 186,000 acres on the adjacent San Juan National Forest. Within a decade more than 250,000 acres of spruce forest were dead. Several years of drought, high temperatures, low humidity, high winds, and lightning set the stage for a *Perfect Storm* in the summer of 2013. Three lightning strikes ignited raging forest fires that consumed nearly 110,000 acres of spruce forest in the Rio Grande and San Juan National Forests.

Fire fighters performed a Herculean task of protecting structures and private property. When the flames died and monsoon rains began, new life immediately began to spring from the ashes. Although it is most saddening to witness the destruction of such magnitude, it is exciting to have survived it. This generation and those following are going to witness the rebirth of land and forest.

There is a deep desire within all of us to protect a forest as generations before us did. Because trees don't move, we come to think of them as being permanent fixtures of the landscape. The landscape will change with new gullies, landslides and debris flows for the next few years. Nature has no concern for our feelings or values. One year after the fire, grasses were growing in the meadows; forbs have sprouted in some of the burned areas. Aspen were sprouting in abundance. Some areas however, burned with such intensity and heat, that they could take centuries to recover. In the near future the nutrients in the ash will nurture a resurgence of life on the mountains. The decadent and dead vegetation were consumed. Even the aquatic insect life in the Rio Grande has shown a renewed vigor. The early stages of vegetative succession are the most productive for wildlife. Take heart, there is a silver lining in the ashes of a forest fire.

Those of us who spent so many years riding those now charred drainages cherish the memories of riding through the coolness of tall timber on hot summer days. Fortunately, there are still hundreds of miles of forest trails to ride and hike, streams to fish and wildlife to enjoy. Cherish and protect what is to come.

Mountain Jewels

Writing down the trails of my life has been cathartic. It is impossible to share all the stories and events that I have experienced. My life has never been mundane. So far I haven't written about the little things, the brief moments, and encounters with nature and people that have brought me to the winter of my life. I hope that you have experienced some of these echoes from God's mountains that I cherish:

The whistle of a marmot sentry
A squirrel announcing an intruder
A newborn calf elk
Calf elk frolicking in a mountain meadow
The bugle of a bull elk
Bighorn rams butting heads
A soaring eagle
A beaver splashing its tail
A bear walking up the trail
A mule deer bouncing away in flight
A baby snowshoe hare
Pristine waters of a high mountain lake
White-capped waves driven by the wind
Ripples across a beaver pond

A Cutthroat rising for a fly on a clear mountain stream
Breathtaking expanses of mountain grandeur
Waterfalls that mesmerize the mind
A mountain reflection on a lake
Miniature plants shivering in alpine wind
An old log cabin in the forest
Golden aspen leaves floating like little boats down a creek
The warmth and companionship of a campfire
Flickering flames that soothe the soul
Horse shoes clicking on a rocky trail
Sensing the strength of a horse
Colorado columbine flower gardens
Rain falling and dripping off my hat
A rainbow arching over a mountain valley
Snowflakes silently falling
Petroglyphs carved in stone
Puffy white clouds drifting cross blue sky
Black clouds, lightning, and thunder
Moon light sparkling off a snow covered landscape
A cold crystal-clear spring
Icy wind that chills to the bone
Earthly fragrances drifting on a mountain breeze
Spruce trees that wave in mountain winds
Rocky peaks and spires that point to heaven
Mountain trails paved with golden leaves

And then there were people:
A silver miner with a heart of gold
A sheriff who cared for his people
A rancher who cared for cattle, land, and people
A nurse who cared for people and animals
A mountain man-tougher than nails, gentle as a mountain breeze
A saddle pal
A judge who could scare, care, and be fair
A teacher who inspired students
A handyman who could fix anything
A preacher who lived what he taught
A State Trooper who rode the highways with God
A Boy Scout
A city marshal who was always there
A neighbor

A boss who was patient, caring, and supportive
A stranger who walked through town to a place he didn't know
A counselor who walked along side
A doctor who loved doctoring
A coworker who could criticize me as a friend
Mentors who tutored me through the Bible
A senator with integrity
And so many, many more

There were a few folks who tried to have a negative influence on me. Most were unsuccessful, but memorable. I hold no grudges. I have experienced forgiveness from those whom I have offended and given the same. I have been blessed with people who were patient with me. I've been cursed and hated by more than a few. Those who have been in law enforcement understand. I regret and I'm sorry that I've caused pain to some and hopefully I've comforted more folks than I've offended.

What really matters now

I had the humbling privilege and honor of working alongside some of the finest wildlife professionals throughout my career. There are many monuments that pay tribute to what we accomplished during our watch. It was not just wildlife professionals I worked with, but also citizens representing many interest groups who had a heart for wildlife and contributed in so many ways. They didn't always agree, but we reached consensus to solve problems and maximize the opportunities for wildlife and the environment.

We worked the system within our own agency as well as with other agencies and organizations to accomplish our mission. Personnel behind the scenes were liaisons with legislators, wildlife commissioners, and local governments to enact legislation and regulations to protect and enhance the environment for wildlife.

As I look back now, it is not all our accomplishments, which were many, that seem as important to me. Yes, I'm proud of what we did and the fact that people continue to enjoy the fruits of our labors. What I personally value and cherish the most are the memories of working with all kinds of people and the relationships that we shared. Some relationships were close and personal and others were adversarial, but the all added up to a life that I feel good about.

For Wildlife Officers who are in the saddle now and those to come, it is my hope that you too will continue to have vision. Continue to climb to the top of the mountains and peer across the Divide. Listen to the echoes of the past with respect and appreciate what we did. Our predecessors gave us a legacy of stewardship and we pass it on to you. This goes for the citizens of our country as well. Climb higher, look farther and in a new age of knowledge continue to protect and enhance our wildlife and along the way may you experience that the people you live amongst and the memories you make are what makes life more worthwhile.

.BENEDICTION

Almighty God and Heavenly Father,

Thank you for life
    For all of creation you made
Thank you for revealing yourself in all that is visible and invisible
    For the immenseness of the universe and the tiny things as
        well
Thank you for the experiences of life.
    For those that felt good and for those that were hard
Thank you for the people you brought into my life.
    Those who were kind and those who challenged me
Thank you for your faithfulness and watching over me
    For providing what I needed
Thank you for the United States of America
    For the freedom we cherish
Thank you for your discipline to keep me in your will.
    The forgiveness when I went my own way
Thank you for your mercy that I never did deserve.
    Most of all thank you for your enduring love.
Now I ask you to bless those who remain and those to come.
    Draw them ever closer to yourself and to each other.
AMEN

May God's wild places and His wildlife always
lift your spirit and refresh your soul. .

HAPPY TRAILS TO YOU

"I look to the mountains; does my strength come from mountains? No, my strength comes from God who made heaven, and earth and mountains."

Psalms 121: 1, 2

BIBLIOGRAPHY

Aerial Detection Survey Summary for Rocky Mountain Region of the U.S. Forest Service 2013

Peter and Holmes, Judith, Colorado's Wildlife Story, Colorado Division of Wildlife, 1990

Colorado Supreme Court: Sergent vs The People of Colorado, rehearing, June 12, 1972

Grosz, Terry, The Thin Green Line, Outwitting Poachers, Smugglers & Market Hunters, Flying Pen Press LLC, 2011

Hinshaw, Glen, Crusaders for Wildlife, A History of Wildlife Stewardship in Southwest Colorado, Western Reflections, Lake City, Colorado 2000

Leopold, Aldo, A Sand County Almanac, original copyright 1949, Oxford Press

Peterson, David, Ghost Grizzlies, Johnson Publishing, Boulder, Colorado, 1998

Wikipedia.org/wiki/Minutemen_ (anti-ommunist_organization) 2013

INDEX

ABOUT THE AUTHOR

Glen Hinshaw was born and raised in Denver, Colorado in 1941. He grew up with a Bible in one hand and a fishing pole in the other. As a youth he followed his dad exploring and fishing the high country of the Colorado Rockies. His Christian faith and exposure to the great out-of-doors were the two guiding influences in his life.

As a teenager, Glen set a goal to become a Colorado Wildlife Officer. After graduation from North High School in Denver, he earned a Bachelor of Science degree in Wildlife Management from Colorado State University in 1963. Soon after graduation he achieved his goal as a Wildlife Conservation Officer in the Colorado Game and Fish Department.

Glen was assigned to the Cortez district where he served for three years. In 1966 Glen transferred to the Creede district and served there for nearly twenty-two years. While he was in Creede he was awarded the "Wildlife Officer of the Year" award in 1968 and in 1985 "Conservationist of the Year" award from the Colorado Chapter of Trout Unlimited.

In 1988 Glen was promoted to the Southwest Region's Information and Education Specialist position. That job evolved into his holding several titles and responsibilities. When he retired in 1997 he was the Education Coordinator for Western Colorado.

Toward the end of his tenure he was honored with the Division's "Most Positive Employee" award. In 1997 the Colorado Alliance for Environmental Education gave him "The Enos Mills Lifetime Achievement Award for Environmental Education".

Glen lived a life dedicated to preserving God's wild places and wildlife and as a servant to the people who crossed his trail.